LONDON'S RECORD SHOPS

LONDON'S RECORD SHOPS

TEXT AND SELECT IMAGES BY GARTH CARTWRIGHT
PHOTOGRAPHY BY QUINTINA VALERO

The History Press

First published 2021

The History Press
97 St George's Place, Cheltenham,
Gloucestershire, GL50 3QB
www.thehistorypress.co.uk

British Library Cataloguing in Publication Data.
A catalogue record for this book is available from the British Library.

ISBN 978 0 7509 9604 4

Typesetting and origination by The History Press
Printed and bound in Turkey by Imak.

CONTENTS

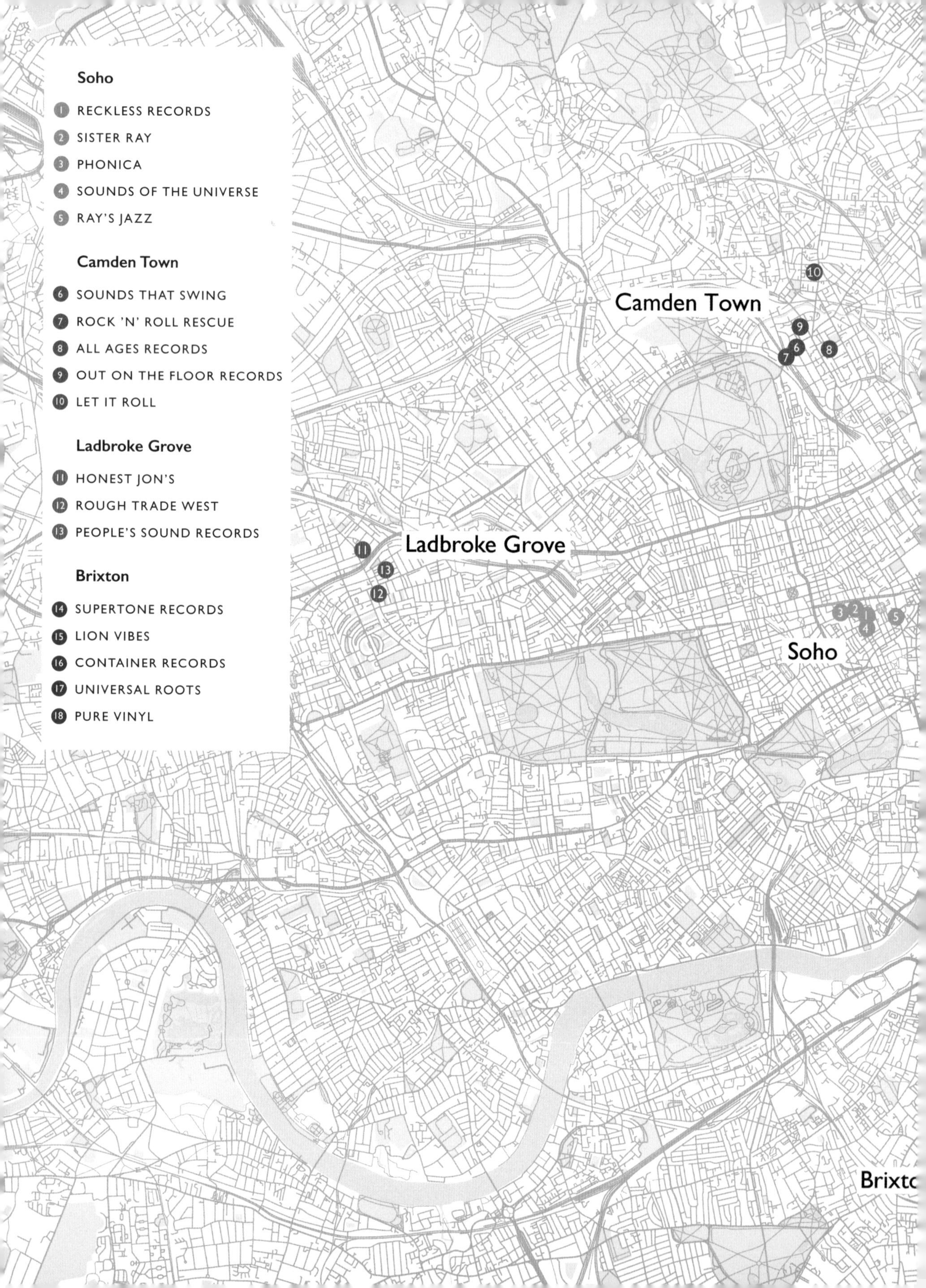
Soho
1 RECKLESS RECORDS
2 SISTER RAY
3 PHONICA
4 SOUNDS OF THE UNIVERSE
5 RAY'S JAZZ
Camden Town
6 SOUNDS THAT SWING
7 ROCK 'N' ROLL RESCUE
8 ALL AGES RECORDS
9 OUT ON THE FLOOR RECORDS
10 LET IT ROLL
Ladbroke Grove
11 HONEST JON'S
12 ROUGH TRADE WEST
13 PEOPLE'S SOUND RECORDS
Brixton
14 SUPERTONE RECORDS
15 LION VIBES
16 CONTAINER RECORDS
17 UNIVERSAL ROOTS
18 PURE VINYL
Camden Town
Ladbroke Grove
Soho

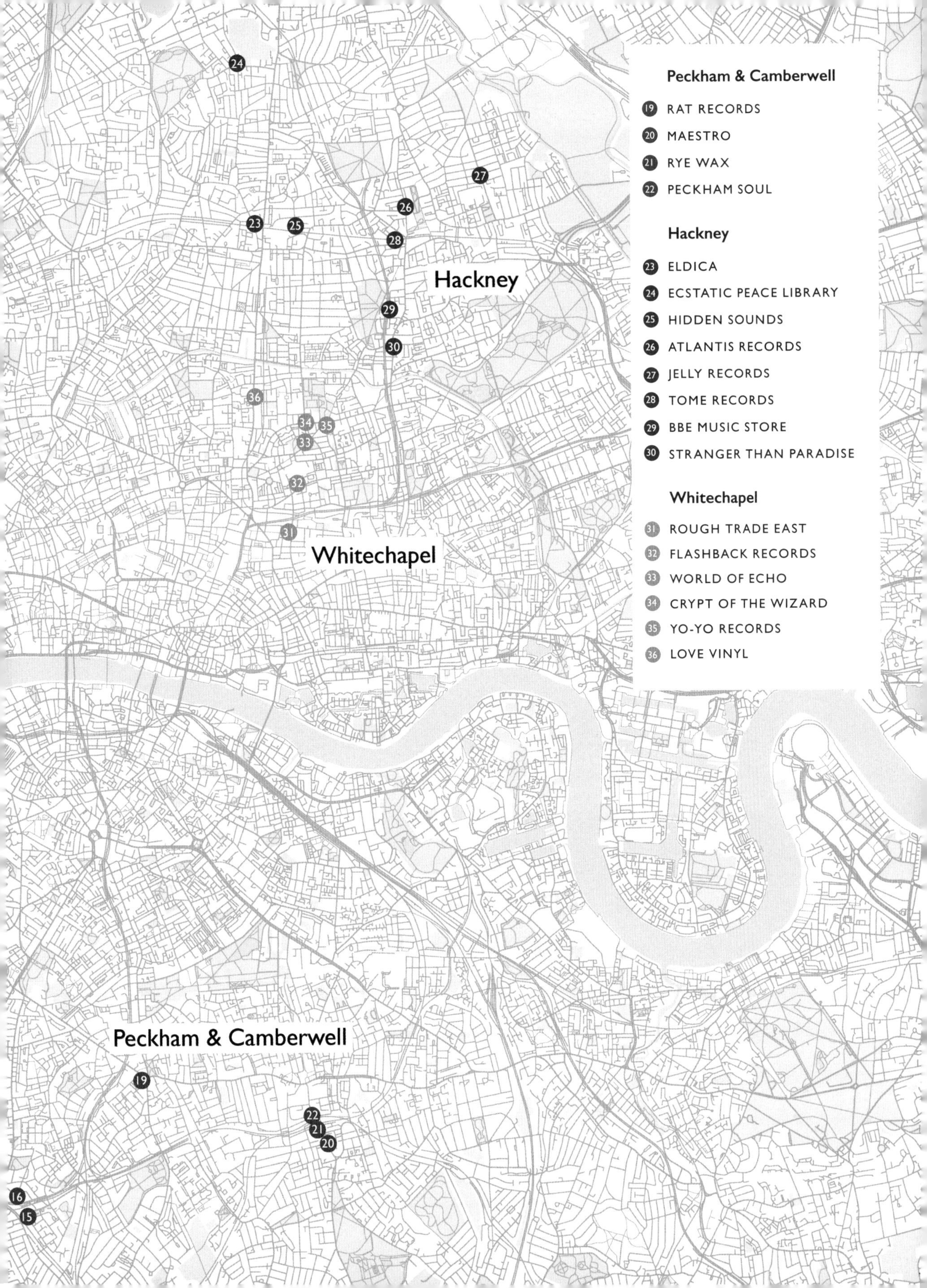
Peckham & Camberwell
19 RAT RECORDS
20 MAESTRO
21 RYE WAX
22 PECKHAM SOUL
Hackney
23 ELDICA
24 ECSTATIC PEACE LIBRARY
25 HIDDEN SOUNDS
26 ATLANTIS RECORDS
27 JELLY RECORDS
28 TOME RECORDS
29 BBE MUSIC STORE
30 STRANGER THAN PARADISE
Whitechapel
31 ROUGH TRADE EAST
32 FLASHBACK RECORDS
33 WORLD OF ECHO
34 CRYPT OF THE WIZARD
35 YO-YO RECORDS
36 LOVE VINYL
Hackney
Whitechapel
Peckham & Camberwell
15
16

FOREWORD BY CORNERSHOP

We were lucky enough to have started our group, Cornershop, on Wiiija Records, the name being the postcode W11 1JA of the owners, Rough Trade record shop, Portobello, London. We spent many happy days in their basement & forecourt. That was an education of how a marvellous record shop worked: great one-to-one with customers, enthusiastic independent stocking, regulars, out-of-towners (and out-of-countryers), great conversation, a wonderful tea and coffee-making area – and the truth.

Every record is a truth, and that's the beauty of these vinyl medicinal libraries. In there is what the world is about, will be about and should be about, even if you have to turn a message upside down or shake it, to find your own truth. We have all heard tales of going into record shops that are as daunting as going to the dentist to be ridiculed for your lack of mouth hygiene. My advice is to walk out of such shops, and walk straight back in again, because even a shop assistant on a bad day is part of the truth and so is your determination to find it.

Tjinder Singh
(singer, songwriter, producer)

As a teenager my criteria for visiting anywhere were based entirely on whether it had any decent record shops or not. I'd avoid towns if I discovered they had none. I figured if a place didn't have a good record shop then it wasn't worth visiting, there had to be something wrong with it and its people.

Naturally, London was quite an attraction. In 1983, aged 15, with an hour to myself to explore I discovered a small, darkly lit, used record shop on Hanway Street, just off Oxford Street. The selection inside blew my mind. It seemed like another world and the experience set something off inside me. I've basically sought out these places ever since.

Whenever touring with Cornershop, between the bus arriving at the venue and stage time, we'd always go and find the best local record shops. One place in San Francisco – where we had to crawl over boxes to get to more boxes of records – often springs to mind. It was always an adventure and an education.

The best thing about a good record shop is that you can walk out with something you had no idea you were looking for – and it could turn out to be the best record you've ever heard. I love the randomness and unpredictability of it, it makes the experience constantly intriguing. The thing is, every record shop has its regulars, and they provide an important point of human interaction for all of them, they're crucial social hubs to so many.

The original Ladbroke Grove Rough Trade was a meeting place for so many great musicians, fanzine writers, punk and reggae groups. Everyone, from Nikki Sudden of Swell Maps to Adele, has worked behind the counter there. I've since discovered the place on Hanway Street would have been Rocks Off, where Shane MacGowan worked.

In the past it was often hard to find these places. This book guides you on a personal tour around the remaining (and new) record shops in London and you can't beat that. It also has heaps of historical information about London's lost record shops. These are magical places – go and visit them all.

Ben Ayres
(guitar, tamboura)

INTRODUCTION

Whether epic, operatic endeavours – from Handel's 'Messiah' to Queen's 'Bohemian Rhapsody', voices from the underclass (measure the gap between John Gay's 'Beggar's Opera' and Stormzy's 'Heavy Weighs the Head'), or the endearing cheeky charm that many a singer has served up (think Noel Coward and Marc Bolan, Boy George and Little Simz), London throbs with music. This ancient city of song enchanting listeners worldwide since time out of mind.

Indeed, anyone who spends long enough in the city they call 'the Smoke' will realise how the music made here is all part of a river of song that winds its way through the centuries, shape-shifting and morphing, an intrinsic part of London's psychic atmosphere. Broadsheet ballads morphed into Cockney singsongs into Lionel Bart's urchin psalms, Small Faces' lad anthems, Sex Pistols' angry polemic, Ian Dury's geezer wit, Smiley Culture's sound system chat and on into grime's urban narratives.

Being home to people from across the globe ensures that the UK's capital city serves as a laboratory for all kinds of sonic experiments. Irish fiddlers and Jewish klezmer singers once rubbed shoulders in crowded tenements, Madness sang ska tunes as shaped by Kentish Town's council estates, while Soul II Soul – from neighbouring Camden Town – gave the Jamaican sound system a pop styling.

This is a city whose suburbs have produced an array of distinctive female singers: the likes of Dusty Springfield, Sandie Shaw, Helen Shapiro, Linda Lewis, Kate Bush, Amy Winehouse and Adele grew up in myriad London postcodes, all making remarkably individual music. Formidable tower blocks serve as incubators for urban music as hard as the concrete that housed its creators. A Notting Hill Carnival city. A jazz city. A West End musical city. A rock city. A rave city. A classical and an opera city. A city where music is constantly being created, brought/bought, remodelled/reissued. Many outsiders – and likely a few locals – imagine music exists in the very air that Londoners breathe, beats emanating from the streets, a budding star on every stage.

If the reality isn't quite so fabulous, it's fair to describe London as one of the world's great music cities. Alongside the music being made here, from the late nineteenth century until the early twenty-first century, London proudly served as Europe's foremost record shop city. Admittedly, US retail culture and independent record label milieu ensured, across the first half of the twentieth century, that New York City and New Orleans, Los Angeles and Chicago had record shops like nowhere else. But the 1960s found Londoners, never keen on doffing their collective cap, opening vinyl emporiums offering many different genres of music alongside a real hunger to get new sounds heard: no other city had the record shop mash-up of pop and rock, Jamaican and Indian, Turkish and Greek, Jewish and jazz, punk and techno, which would take fabulously unruly shape across the Smoke.

London is where HMV, the world's foremost record shop chain, began with a single outlet on Oxford Street in 1921. A quarter of a century later Dobell's, the foremost jazz/blues/folk record shop, opened on Charing Cross Road, serving as a magnet for musicians for decades to come: the likes of Louis Armstrong and B.B. King held court here, while a young (and stoned) Bob Dylan recorded in its basement one freezing January night in 1963.

London is where Richard Branson began to build his empire by opening the very first of his Virgin enterprises – a threadbare hippie hangout above a discount shoe shop – in January 1971 (again, on Oxford Street). Five years later, Geoff Travis would open Rough Trade in Ladbroke Grove, which was then an impoverished West Indian neighbourhood. Around the same time, another small chain of London records shops developed a record label as a sideline: after opening several Beggars Banquet shops across south-west London, owner Martin Mills started a record label to issue a 45 by a punk band no one else would touch. Today, the Beggars Group of labels is the world's most powerful independent record label conglomerate: Gary Numan, The Pixies, The Prodigy, Adele and many others owe their careers to Mills deciding he could run a label out of his Fulham shop's basement.

That Virgin, Rough Trade and the Beggars Banquet record labels grew out of independent London record shops, all founded by young men determined to champion the music they and their peers loved, demonstrates how visionary these record shops – and their very different owners – were. These examples might appear remarkable but – *get this!* – they're not the first: in the 1920s, Levy's of Whitechapel set up the Levaphone and Oriole labels to issue records for both the area's Jewish community and jazz fans, while Dobell's started 77 Records in the 1950s to get blues and folk records released (one LP featured the aforementioned, stoned, soon-to-be-superstar folk singer).

Back in the early '60s Transat Imports, in a Soho basement, imported the hottest new R&B 45s. Regular customers would include members of the Stones, Small Faces and other game-changing rock bands. In the mid-1960s, ground-breaking reggae label Trojan Records got started as an offshoot of the Muzik City record shops that Lee Gopthal opened across London to sell Jamaican records.

Goth pioneers Bauhaus and The Cure both issued their debut 45s on Small Wonder, a tiny punk label run out of a tiny punk record shop in Walthamstow. Rock On went from a market stall to Camden Town's greatest-ever record shop and birthed Ace Records, the world's foremost reissue label of rock 'n' roll and R&B. Stern's African Record Shop, nestled behind Warren Street Station, began a record label to ensure African music got heard.

Myriad dance music genres have been formulated in record shops, from Black Market developing UK house in Soho, and Big Apple shaping dubstep in Croydon to Rhythm Division helming grime in Hackney. Several former dance shop employees would go on to enjoy lucrative careers as DJs.

London is a city of huge energies and enterprise and the capital's record shops have always reflected this in their energy and enterprise. A good record shop exists to do far more than simply sell products to punters. Instead, they serve as community spaces, energy magnets, meeting houses, places where friendships are forged, bands formed, labels launched; creative hubs that are part of an underground empire trafficking in joy.

Yet, at the start of the twenty-first century things began to fall apart. No one predicted such, but in the noughties, a slow and then sudden change hit the city's record shops and they began to topple. A perfect storm of supermarket chains selling chart CDs as loss leaders, the rapid rise of Amazon selling VAT-free CDs, illegal downloading and file sharing (combined with inflated high street rents), spelt doom for many of London's record shops. Just as video rental shops had rapidly vanished from the high street, so it seemed would the record shop.

By 2009, an air of ruination haunted the streets as record shop after record shop turned off the music, boxed the remaining stock and locked their doors for the final time. It was if an invisible virus – felling everyone from the mighty Tower and Virgin chains to long-standing independents like Dub Vendor and Mole Jazz – had decimated the trade.

For those of us who love record shops, the mass closures were a retail tragedy. Arriving in the Smoke in 1991, I was awed at the riches on offer. Dominating Piccadilly Circus stood Europe's biggest record shop, the three-storey Tower Records; Ray's Jazz sat on Shaftesbury Avenue, the toast of the Soho jazz scene; while in nearby Berwick Street (and the streets immediately off it) there were up to twenty-four independent record shops operating. HMV and Virgin Megastores dominated Oxford Street. Camden Town, Brixton and Ladbroke Grove also offered a smorgasbord of shops to sift through – Camden offering all kinds of rock, Brixton being strongly Jamaican, the Grove eclectic and electric.

Actually, record shops were everywhere: Harlesden was home to myriad reggae shops, while down in leafy Kingston half a dozen different emporiums coexisted on the high street. Croydon had Beano's – Europe's largest used record shop – and dance music shops that served pirate radio. Branches of Virgin, HMV and Our Price could be found alongside the independent shops. Offbeat specialists – soundtracks, rockabilly, psychedelia, heavy rock, classical, African, Latin – were tucked away on quiet suburban streets.

And then the cull began. Among the first casualties was Our Price, the 300-plus-strong chain of chart CD record shops that had existed on every high street in the UK. Richard Branson, aware of the downward spiral, rebranded all his Virgin record shops as Zavvi: within eighteen months the entire chain had collapsed. Tower retreated across the Atlantic but this didn't save the USA's most successful record retail chain.

Left: *Decca Gramophone advertisement.*

Below: *International Bookshop advertisement.*

Don't hesitate . . .

to visit us if you want jazz records. We have them on every label, on all speeds and to suit the taste of anyone keen on traditional Modern, modern Traditional, or just plain Middle-of-the-road. If you want to read about jazz, then look through our selection of jazz books and magazines—the widest choice in London (send for our book-list if you can't come personally).

Second-hand discs. World wide postal service.

MEMBER OF J.R.R.A.

THE INTERNATIONAL BOOKSHOP

52Charing Cross Rd,, London W.C.2. Telephone: Tem 2351

From 1970 to the 1990s Woolworths had been the UK's premier retailer of 45s, selling literally millions and millions of smash hits, but not a single 'Woolies' survives. HMV closed dozens of stores, here and abroad. Northern record shop chains MVC, Music Zone and Fopp all fell apart, with only Fopp – who had London outlets – surviving (a handful out of what had been close to 100 stores).

Berwick Street and its environs also suffered: the youth were no longer crowding in to buy new dance and reggae singles, nor excited by the release of new indie rock albums or imports of US underground artists. And who wanted to buy a used CD? From paying £15 for a new release CD, HMV was now offering them at £10 while 'classic' albums were reissued cheaply: seminal jazz and blues, soul and rock CDs could be found retailing at £5 (or less) brand new. That is, if you still bought music. Many youths decided they preferred to listen on their phones while newly computer literate adults joined their kids in downloading new and old favourites. To many observers it looked like 'game over' for record retail.

For the chains it appeared so but the votary continued, desperate spiritual outlaws, refusing to quit, intoxicated by the music they traded in – most notably, Rough Trade East opened in 2007 and, right from the start, was a success. Incorporating a café and a stage (for live performances by visiting musicians), alongside large selections of vinyl and CDs, books and magazines, East possessed a real sense of bonhomie and excitement about contemporary music. Here was a record shop that existed because it believed in sharing music with music lovers rather than a megastore trying to sell shedloads of chart CDs (as Virgin, Tower, HMV, Our Price, etc. had all devolved into). It proved to be what music lovers wanted.

Rough Trade East (and West) proudly waved the flag for London as a record shop city. Others would follow in their wake, and the new shops are often opening in areas whose last record shop was an Our Price in the 1990s. Instead of following video rental into extinction, London's record shops are enjoying a glorious resurrection.

This resurrection was brought about by a psychic shift that few predicted. A sudden – and unexpected – surge in enthusiasm for vinyl saved many independent record shops. Initially, this appeared to be a reaction to downloading music: middle-aged music fans decided their favourite albums looked (and sounded) better on vinyl so started buying LPs again while, around the same time, youths who had only known their parents' CD collections (alongside downloading the music they liked), found in vinyl a hip, vintage artefact. If the oldies wanted new copies of their favourite rock and jazz LPs, the youngsters desired 7 and 12 inch 45s by the bands and DJs they followed. Like the slow food movement, vinyl became about taking the time to listen seriously to music again – the opposite of the sonic indigestion that having too much music available via your computer offers.

Around the same time as the vinyl revival took hold, Record Store Day (RSD) began to gain prominence. First launched in the USA to draw attention to the surviving record stores there, RSD quickly caught on in the UK, ensuring labels who had dismissed vinyl for decades (as they minted fortunes from the CD boom) suddenly began rushing out all kinds of tosh on LP. Still, the event drew plenty of attention to surviving independent record shops – not that all of them wanted to participate; some of London's most established independent record shops scorn RSD.

London's new record shop landscape is, in many ways, very different from that of the old. People who only bought a couple of albums a year were never going to return to record shops – the supermarkets and Amazon serve their needs – or they stopped buying music altogether. Physical sales of singles and albums have fallen massively across this century and the recent upturn in vinyl sales (LPs and 45s having been relegated to a very niche format across the 1990s by major labels intent on profiting from CDs) has not made up for the loss in income.

Thus, there will never be another music megastore – even HMV closed its historic 363 Oxford Street shop in January 2018. Today No. 363 is marked only by a bronze plaque noting how The Beatles' manager, Brian Epstein, secured his band a recording deal with EMI via his contacts – Brian being the manager of NEMS, Liverpool's foremost record shop in the 1950s–60s – in the Oxford Street shop.

HMV is the only record shop chain left standing, but it now has little presence in London and no shop in the West End (outside of Fopp in Covent Garden, which it owns). HMV's only London branches today are in Bromley, Romford and Westfield Shopping Centre. The chain's retreat, while independent record shops rise, is a reflection of who and how recorded music is bought today. Those who venture into record shops are music obsessives, not excited tweens spending their pocket money on a new heart-throb or people popping in to buy something they heard on the Radio 1 *Breakfast Show*. What marks the Smoke's record shops today are independent traders, both established and newbies, who 'curate' the music they stock to ensure those who come to browse find all kinds of treasure.

London's twenty-first-century record shops are, for the most part, reflective of how rich and varied the Smoke's music culture is. Jazz, dance, electronica, underground rock, folk, reggae, soul, rap, African, Latin, punk, metal, rockabilly and psychedelic rarities have all found receptive vendors. At the same time, classical/opera have suffered from a lack of enthusiasm, with the last two of central London's classical shops – Soho's Harold Moore's and Waterloo's Gramex – both shutting in 2017. Pop and urban releases are now designed to be consumed via streaming services, so don't expect to easily pick up new vinyl or CD releases by, say, Rita Ora or Headie One. The era of popping into Woolies for chart bangers is as extinct as the chain itself.

While researching this book in early 2020, the COVID-19 pandemic hit, forcing all 'non-essential' shops into lockdown. This meant that for three months no records were sold across counters (or at street markets or record fairs) for the first time since the 78 shellac disc became available in 1902. Yet demand remained strong: shops that had a strong online presence – Honest Jon's and Rough Trade – found they were selling remarkable numbers via mail order. Many smaller traders

Stuart Baker, Soul Jazz impresario, Soho.

Above: *Hand-painted dividers designed by Ski Williams.*
Below: ***Becky Fox, Camden Town..***

went onto Discogs and managed to sustain themselves there. But the news from the USA was awful: Amoeba Music ran a crowdfunding campaign to keep its Sunset Strip megastore viable then announced the inevitable closure, while historic shops from Record Mart (Manhattan's oldest record store) to Seattle's Bop Street Records all gave up the ghost. How hard, we wondered, would London be hit?

As of writing – autumn 2020 – not as hard as feared. There have been a handful of closures, yet these are, more often than not, due to rapacious landlords hiking the rent. Overall, traders are cautiously positive, with London's newest record shops (Hidden Sounds and Atlantis Records in Hackney, Lorenzo's in Brockley, Next Door Records in Shepherds Bush) all up and at it. With record shops no longer common on the high street they are now niche businesses, a blend of vintage/junk shop and art gallery. I wander into them looking for everyday magic and engage in myriad delights.

Today's surviving shops are often quirky, even eccentric. Mercifully, the dust and rudeness that characterised certain traders is now largely absent. Indeed, I'd venture that, while there are far fewer record shops than twenty years ago, the quality and bonhomie is often superior today. Less is more? Something like that. Those who run/work in shops in 2020 do it because they love music with a huge passion. A vocation? Indeed.

So, to this book. A celebration of London's surviving record shops at the dawn of the 2020s. While I will reference the pioneering shops, this isn't a social history (my 2018 book *Going for a Song: A Chronicle of the UK Record Shop* serves that purpose). Nor does this book attempt to document every London record shop currently trading – instead, I've concentrated on a selection of London neighbourhoods that are abuzz with record shops. While the likes of Soho and Camden have long offered crate-digging delights, there's been a startling resurgence in East and South London, reflecting the demographic changes under way in many London neighbourhoods over the past fifteen years. Other areas remain bereft of record shops: from Balham to the Walworth Road, none now exist. While Finchley/Golders Green has one shop (Alan's – he also cuts keys), the King's Road and Mayfair, hotspots during the 1960s–70s, have long been without a single music boutique.

As a lifelong crate digger, I'm happiest when I can wander (or cycle) from one shop to another. Thus, photographer Quintina Valero and I chose to explore these bits of London where there still is a record shop culture of sorts. No offence intended if your favourite shop is not here – there are superb record shops in Greenwich (Casbah), Kingston upon Thames (Banquet), Upminster (Crazy Beat), Ealing (Sounds Original), Twickenham (Eel Pie), Walthamstow (Vinyl Vault), Harlesden (Hawkeye), Shepherds Bush (Peckings), Crystal Palace (Sound Vinyl), Putney (Soul Brother), Mortlake (Level Crossing) and elsewhere. However, this time around, they were too far to cycle to. Here, we lurk around the myriad record shop delights of London's zones 1–2, focusing on the most historic and distinctive, exotic and eccentric.

In 2020, London is proudly Europe's record shop capital. Paris offers rich – if often pricey – pickings; Lisbon has a handful of emporiums; Athens and Brussels, Berlin and Barcelona all have a few fine shops; while the street markets of Tbilisi are packed with traders trying to offload old Deep Purple and Uriah Heep LPs; but back in the UK there is no competition. Birmingham, England's second city, only has two or three record shops; Liverpool and Manchester are somewhat more vigorous but, considering their pedigree, a shadow of their former selves; both Brighton and Edinburgh possess brilliantly quirky vinyl victuallers. Further afield, I've found Auckland and Melbourne, Tokyo and Bangkok, New Orleans and Los Angeles all to be homes to record shops of distinction. But London heaves with great record shops – so much so that no US city now matches it.

Time, then, to celebrate the Smoke and the fabulous music emporiums that help enliven our city. Good digging, y'all!

Garth Cartwright, SE15

SOHO

RECKLESS RECORDS
SISTER RAY
PHONICA
SOUNDS OF THE UNIVERSE (SOTU)
RAY'S JAZZ

There's something unique about Soho. Upon entering its fabled streets I experience a psychic sense of a neighbourhood possessing its own micro-climate, more humid and edgy than that found outside its borders. Because there is no public transport within this warren of narrow streets and alleys (so forcing visitors to find their own way in and around), its character – very London and very cosmopolitan – has retained something now lost across much of the West End. Indeed, the tourist hordes who invade the surrounding streets rarely venture in, while lingering traces of a sex industry (and the villains who fed off it) add a different kind of tension. Soho's buzzy energy and somewhat seedy atmosphere ensures it remains unlike anywhere else.

At least since the end of the Second World War, Soho existed as the epicentre of the UK's record shop trade. There's little documentation for prior decades but, situated in the heart of the West End and home to all kinds of clubs – from private members to jazz (where visiting musicians would gather to blow with the locals) to secret gay clubs (simply attending such carried the threat of imprisonment until homosexuality was decriminalised in 1967) – plus countless pubs, record labels, music publishers' offices and such suggests this was the case.

Prior to HMV opening at 363 Oxford Street as a specialist record/gramophone dealer, many of the large West End stores had gramophone departments. Here you could buy both equipment and records. Depending on how luxurious the store was they might have offered a listening room where equipment and records could be demonstrated in optimum conditions.

Among the most noted department stores for music were Imhof's at 112 New Oxford Street, which first opened in 1883 (and began selling wax cylinder playing phonographs in 1896) and was celebrated for supplying the royal family with gramophones and 78s. Even in the 1960s, Imhof's Record Bar – as these emporiums were often called – was noted for its US imports and deep stock.

The huge Gramage Store at 128 Holborn had a gramophone department (along with much else on offer), while Selfridge's department store at 400 Oxford Street opened in 1909 and its American owner ensured it had an excellent gramophone department and 78 selection. Less ostentatious, but very effective, was the chain of Keith Prowse ticket agencies: these sold 78s alongside concert/theatre tickets across London – their hub being Coventry Street.

By the 1920s, specialist record shops were all over the West End, with Rimington Van

Vintage Glamour Mama holding her favourite Bowie LP on Berwick Street.

Wyck Ltd on Cranbourne Street (a highbrow shop whose 78 sleeves boasted 'Gramophone Music for the Connoisseur'), while Levy's – who feature in the Whitechapel section – operated a shop at 94–96 Regent Street. EMG's gramophone salon on Grape Street was noted for both its acoustic gramophones (very useful in the colonies) and snooty clerks.

The Gramophone Exchange on Shaftesbury Avenue was one of the first and most celebrated of London record shops – it existed until 2017 (admittedly, its final years were played out in a small shop behind Waterloo Station). Back then, almost all record shops had listening booths – you would request a record to listen to and the clerk would assign you a booth where to do so, a private pleasure many indulged in while out shopping.

To get an idea of Soho shellac shopping before the rock era, we have the reminisces of Ronald Hastings, which were shared with *Gramophone Magazine* in November 1986 (c/o Gramex's website www.gramex.co.uk):

> *In 1940, my regular record gathering programme commenced with the purchase of a 1s. 6d. return workman's ticket very early on a Saturday morning. Then there followed a day of record (listening) before returning with, usually, two new discs, carefully chosen after hearing as many as I thought I could get away with, and still be welcome in the same shops the following week. Arriving at Charing Cross from Kent before 8 a.m., so that the ticket was still legal, one walked everywhere. First of all up to the old and great Gramophone Exchange, at that time in large premises on two floors in upper Shaftesbury Avenue. At one time the main, ground floor was for new records, the basement for secondhand, but the two got mixed up over the years. 'Pop' Russell ran it and tall Bill Snow sat by the window behind the counter. Some years later they moved to Wardour Street which I never liked so much. We were reluctant to take records in for sale to stern looking Mr Russell. At the far end of the earlier shop were those listening booths, musical retreats we all loved so much (except when other people opened the door with the same inquiry you got in phone booths). For each record I intended to buy I reckoned to hear three. In this way much time passed, except at HMV — at that time a fine, classical shop in Oxford Street (same position as now) — where they were a bit 'stuffy' if you played records right through and would often insist that you didn't. Heaven for me was when I discovered the hidden EMG shop. This was tucked away in Grape Street, a small turning off Shaftesbury Avenue, so only a few yards from The Gramophone Exchange. At EMG you could only buy new discs, but they kept many records from the HMV and Columbia Special List and other foreign lists (notably the German and Italian) as well and, above all, would give you advice, the assistants knowing their repertoire—and knowing they knew it!*

The Second World War hit record shops hard: no imported 78s from the USA or the Continent, and shellac could be melted down to make machine oil, so people were encouraged to donate their records to the war effort, while HMV's celebrated basement got turned into a bomb shelter! After the war, the UK suffered extreme austerity with sales tax of up to 80 or 90 per cent levied on records (as 'luxury items'), so making the purchase of 78s very pricey indeed. This ensured record shops only slowly began to return to their pre-war glory.

A new model of record shop developed when Doug Dobell started to sell used jazz 78s in his father's antiquarian bookshop, Dobell's, on Charing Cross Road, in 1946. Doug soon got rid of the books and went on to develop what would be seen as Soho's foremost jazz/blues/folk record shop. He quickly opened another branch in Rathbone Place and set up a label to issue blues, jazz and folk recordings (often pressing up only ninety-nine copies to avoid sales tax!).

A bit further up Charing Cross Road was Collet's, a radical bookshop that grew out of The International Bookshop – also a jazz 78 stockist, with a basement record bar specialising in folk and jazz. Collet's jazz stock was managed by Ray Smith, who later set up Ray's Jazz on Shaftesbury Avenue, one of the landmark London jazz shops.

Alex Strickland moved from selling records in the back room of his tobacconist on Wardour Street to setting up the Soho Record Centre on the corner of Old Compton and Dean Streets in the late 1950s (from here, he built a London chain of Alex Strickland record shops). Where Dobell's served as a nucleus for jazz, blues and folk fans, the Soho Record Centre specialised in soundtracks to films and musicals and noted Sammy Davis Jr and Frank Sinatra among the celebrities who stepped through its doors.

Laurie Krieger, the founder of Harlequin Records, was less interested in music but very intent on doing business: he opened the first Harlequin in the basement of a stationery shop on Berwick Street in 1961; this possibly being the first record shop on a street now celebrated internationally for its association with the trade. It proved a success and Krieger developed Harlequin into a chain of record shops covering greater London. Krieger would drive around them, collecting takings, in his blue Rolls-Royce.

What exactly turned Berwick Street into the record shop 'royal mile' – actually, more a topped-'n'-tailed kilometre – has never been noted. But many followed Harlequin's lead – the British Record Shop Archive map of Soho's record shops suggested at least thirty different music emporiums have existed, either on Berwick or nearby.

Post-war Soho served as the UK's hotspot for live music. There was jazz at Ronnie Scott's, R&B at the 100 Club, beat bands at The Scene, folk at Les Cousins, while The Marquee began as a jazz and blues venue before becoming the ultimate spot for rising rock bands to prove themselves. There were Italian cafés and restaurants, Jewish tailors and kosher restaurants, Greek delis, eel 'n' pie shops, a horse butcher, merchants with suits and shirts and shoes like you had never seen before, humble haberdasheries selling every make of button, Paul Raymond's Revue Bar offering live striptease shows alongside basement clip joints and brothels tucked into tiny apartments. And pubs, dozens of pubs. Soho served as the UK's most dense business and housing space and, as such, it needed a soundtrack. Berwick Street and its environs provided this.

Wall of vinyl at Phonica.

Kenny Lynch's Record Centre on Walker's Court – linking Berwick Street with Rupert Street – found the self-described 'Black Cockney' pop singer running a very chic shop with listening booths on the walls. The opening of Musicland on Berwick Street in the mid-1960s provided London with its hippest record shop: here were the latest West Coast import albums – the sound of burgeoning psychedelia! A young Elton John loved Musicland so much he would voluntarily work behind the counter when he was not off on tour. Many a budding musician and journalist served time behind the counters at Berwick Street record shops – none quite as famous as Elton, although broadcaster Danny Baker, whose first job after leaving school was at One Stop Records on Berwick Street, certainly knows how to command attention. Danny and Elton both remain record shop devotees but neither has been seen on Berwick Street recently.

The 1980s and '90s were the golden age for the Soho record shop: whether Groove Records on the corner of Greek Street and Bateman Street serving up rap when it was the freshest sound around; or Daddy Kool on Berwick Street blasting dub or Black Market Records on D'Arbly Street, the home of dance music – David Bowie bought his drum and bass 12s here – or Vinyl Junkies providing the city's foremost jazz and funk DJs with the right tunes; or Hitman Records (then Mr Bongo) offering Latin American imports or Ambient Soho for those wanting to chillllllllll. Plus underground rock (Sister Ray, Selectadisc), second-hand (Reckless, Music & Video Exchange, Cheapo Cheapo) and more.

As London property prices have skyrocketed, Soho's been gentrified with long-celebrated shops, pubs and restaurants replaced by caffeine flophouses and branded eateries. Soho is no longer where the mavericks and madmen go to meet; today, it's more likely executives with expense accounts. This noted, I still venture into Soho whenever I'm in the West End, its siren call ensuring I return again and again.

Today, only Ronnie Scott's and the 100 Club survive from when Soho served as an epicentre for live music. Writing while the pandemic still rages, I know both venues want to reopen. Soho without music venues and record shops, well, it's worse than the Tower without ravens, a hint the metropolis is afflicted – urban heart disease, a cultural death of sorts.

Consider how, in recent years, Soho has lost The Astoria, The Borderline and The 12 Bar (all remarkable places to hear live music) alongside record, book and hardware shops, haberdasheries, independent cafés, basement bars and much else and think of what this says about our city. The West End's character, its ferment – London's *soul* – is shaped and nurtured by independent traders and artists and the people who engage and support them.

This noted, Berwick Street still has two long-standing record shops operating – Reckless Records and Sister Ray – and nearby are Phonica and Sounds Of The Universe.

RECKLESS RECORDS

Reckless Records has always dealt in second-hand and continues to offer deep stock (largely LPs with plenty of 45s, alongside a high-quality CD selection). Fair prices and friendly staff all ensure it is a favourite. I picked up LPs by The Fatback Band and Mose Allison last time I popped in and almost never leave empty-handed: from 50p 45s to LPs costing close to £100, Reckless always has gems.

Reckless Records has been managed by Duncan Kerr since it first opened in 1984. Kerr also plays guitar in The Darts and The Brainiac 5. Like his shop, he's helpful, enthusiastic and engaging.

Digging for records at Reckless Records, Soho.

DUNCAN KERR

How did Reckless come to open on Berwick Street?

'Reckless opened first in Islington in 1983 and was an immediate success, so we were soon looking for a shop in the West End. Back then there were at least ten record shops trading in this part of Soho, so we joined them. Soho was really different then to now – much scruffier and the sex industry was still evident then.'

Why has Reckless survived when many of your competitors have closed?

'The reason Reckless thrived was that we were prepared to pay more to customers for decent-quality records, and we turned down rubbish. That gave us a good reputation at a time when music formats were changing over to CDs in the late '80s, and we always looked for good vinyl. Our shops were tidier and less offhand with customers. Over the years a lot of knowledgeable staff have come and gone, with some opening their own shops, several of which are still thriving. We stock a very wide selection of different types of music, from the 1950s to the present day but with far less from recent years because it exists in much smaller quantities. Mostly we sell second-hand records in very good condition alongside a good selection of new vinyl reissues of classic albums from rock, jazz, blues, soul, R&B, hip hop, and the different dance and electronic music of the '80s/'90s.

'We had the good fortune to find a good location in Soho. We chose a bad location to open a Reckless in Camden, down towards Mornington Crescent tube station, twenty years ago and it almost finished the business by losing more money than the other three shops (two in Soho, one in Angel) could support. Soho has always been good for us for tourism, now more than ever, and having Sister Ray, Sounds of the Universe and Phonica close by is brilliant as they are great record shops. Rents are too high to imagine other rivals opening up but it's still pretty good. We'll have to adapt again if Brexit hurts tourism in the UK.'

How did lockdown affect Reckless?

'Like the Phoney War in late 1939, everyone knew that the lockdown was coming but nobody seemed to believe it until the middle of March, at which point everything collapsed at once for retail trade, public transport, music gigs, cinema, theatre and all things social. Reckless Records heaved a sigh of relief when the government somewhat unexpectedly came up with hugely costly support for business and employees. We completely shut up shop and staff discovered that the savings from public transport, lunch and no tempting records to buy meant that a home holiday wasn't so bad after all. After a few weeks, it became obvious that nothing was likely to be the same again, given the likely restrictions of social contact and distancing in small, crowded shops. A major redesign of our shop layout was drawn up and carried out by a contractor and a decorator while staff contributed plenty

Reckless Records' manager Duncan Kerr, Berwick Street, Soho.

of ideas. We aimed for reopening in early August, so we were caught out when retailers were allowed to open in early July. However, the West End remained a ghost town throughout July, with few Soho companies asking staff to return to work yet, thereby removing lunchtime regulars from record shops, not to mention West End shoppers steering clear of public transport, and virtually no tourists to boost sales.

'We opened on August 1st, with a safer shop layout and with most second-hand vinyl records now out on sale in their sleeves, reducing time for staff to process stock and to serve customers. We've overhauled our social networks and we're putting a lot more stock online, but we aim to offer our best stock to our loyal shop customers first before putting it online. The first few days have been much more promising than some of us had expected. The main concern must be a return of lockdowns. Sometimes I wonder how, when, or if record shops will disappear completely, but they keep opening up in the most unexpected places with eager proprietors and keen staff. We'll be doing our best to keep up the tradition in Soho. Many of us don't know what else to do anyway!'

As a record shop veteran, do you see a future for such in London?

'The market in second-hand records and CDs is tiny in this Spotify age, and most young people don't buy anything physical like vinyl and CDs, so they are cutting the links with the past by not browsing and buying records. Having said that, there are a lot of record collections still waiting to come on to the market as those old guys go to the Holy Jukebox in the sky!'

Above: *Tilly Tappenden digs in Reckless.*

Below: *Ben Phillipson, a musician and employee at Reckless Records, holds his favourite album, Scott 4.*

The Meyer Dancers are obsessed with records, in particular 1960s/70s music. They make regular trips to the Soho area to find records to dance to.

SISTER RAY

Across Berwick Street from Reckless sits Sister Ray Records (SRR). Founded by Phil Barton, he launched Sister Ray initially as a stall in Camden Market in 1984. Named after the Velvet Underground's most relentless slice of aggressive speedfreak white noise, he opened his shop in Berwick Street in 1989. Originally, Sister Ray stocked music largely made by noisy bands that listed Lou Reed's misfits as a major influence, much of its stock being devoted to indie/punk/shoegazing/post-rock/experimental.

The building of a hotel complex forced Barton to shift up Berwick and change focus. Today, Sister Ray is no longer the confrontational rock shop of yore – as the market for new rock releases faded, Barton reinvented Sister Ray as a used LP emporium (with an emphasis on 1960s/1970s rock). Upon entering, you find a rather thin selection of rock CDs alongside discounted music books. Head downstairs to a vinyl basement full of new and used LPs (walls are covered with pricey collectors' LPs), plus a small selection of 45s. Sister Ray serves as the West End locus for Record Store Day: people queue outside for hours to gain admission so to purchase RSD-only releases and – in a non-pandemic year – they sell more vinyl on that day than in the run-up to Christmas.

For several years, a minute's walk away from SRR found If Music, a Black music (jazz, soul, funk, reggae) specialist, existing up several flights of stairs (you had to ring the buzzer to gain entry) on D'Arbly Street. A visit there meant you would 'experience' proprietor Jean Claude Thompson's thoughts on music, society, DJs, reissues and much else. He liked to speak his mind, did Jean Claude. The pandemic forced If's closure – along with all other record shops – but when Thompson hoped to reopen in July his landlord hit him with a huge rent increase. He had no option but, for the foreseeable future, to trade online (https://ifmusic.co.uk/).

Phonica Records' manager, Simon Rigg.

PHONICA

Another minute's walk takes you to Poland Street, where sits the majestic Phonica, the last of the Soho dance music shops. With a wall of 12-inch 45s and a row of Technics turntables for customers to listen on, Phonica is spacious, comfortable and enchanting.

While 12-inch 45s are its main stock, Phonica also has a good selection of 7s, LPs and a range of CDs. Every record available here has been thought about and selected because it will likely appeal to Phonica's customer base. Phonica offers excellent service and is far more welcoming and ambient than I recall most dance music shops being. Phonica not only sells dance music, it also hosts events where top DJs gather to play (and these are streamed via the Internet), so taking the sound of the shop to the world; some of these events are extremely popular and attract large international audiences. A dance music shop that also serves as a club – perfect really. Here I purchased the double CD of Gil Scott-Heron's 'I'm New Here' (Tenth Anniversary Expanded Edition) on a damp February day, previously unaware it had even been issued (no, not the lame 'remix' of the same album).

Phonica has been managed by Simon Rigg since it opened in 2003. He shares his thoughts on why his record shop is now regarded as the world's foremost dance music shop.

SIMON RIGG

You opened Phonica in 2003, just as certain established London record shops were beginning to close: what made you think that Phonica could succeed?

'I think at that time there was a gap for a certain sound that was coming from Germany – Kompakt and Playhouse click house, early minimal and electro house. Also, a lot of dance music shops in Soho specialised in particular niches and I wanted to be less one sub-genre and more all kinds of dance-electronic music including funk/soul/disco/reggae/hip hop/techno/house/electronica, etc.'

Dance music record shops were closing at a furious rate as Phonica got started. Why did so many close yet Phonica succeed?

'I think some shops became associated with a particular sound and maybe didn't evolve or change as tastes changed. Also, rents shot up in Soho and vinyl sales decreased and then, when the credit crunch recession came in, a lot of shops were hit.'

Phonica Records, Poland Street, Soho.

Phonica is a lot more friendly than many dance shops. Did you set out to make Phonica welcoming or is this just fortuitous?

'When we opened, most shops were based on that New York classic dance music record store where the records were behind the counter and you came for your weekly fix, but many customers were intimidated by this and liked the flicking through the racks store. I wanted to combine both, where you could shop by yourself quietly or you could engage with the staff behind the counter and ask for their recommendations.'

Phonica quite often hosts in-store events. What, to you, are a few of the most memorable?

'Oh, too many to mention, from Four Tet's 3-hour sweat-fest' where we had to throw away a few T-shirts as we didn't realise how hot and sweaty it would get in the shop, to our annual Record Store Day events where we get to use the huge space downstairs under the shop with surprise DJs from Chez Damier to Juan Atkins, Midland to DMX Krew, Soulwax to Giles Peterson.'

Soho has always been a music hub: is it still a good place to run a record shop?

'Soho has changed a lot over the last ten years. It's still being gentrified with a new hotel next to the market – and even the Ivy here now! But at least there's still many independent stores, including the very best, reliable record stores: Phonica, Sister Ray, Reckless and Sounds of the Universe.'

Sounds of the Universe on Broadway Street, Soho.

SOUNDS OF THE UNIVERSE (SOTU)

Back across Berwick Street, then left on to Broadwick Street, you arrive at Sounds Of The Universe (SOTU). Here Soul Jazz Records – a superb record label that specialises in reissuing rare yet wonderful music from New Orleans, Jamaica, Nigeria, Brazil and other temperate regions of the planet – operates. In this sense, Sounds Of The Universe echoes Vogue Records, a 1950s-era jazz label and namesake record shop that existed on the fringes of Soho. Alongside Soul Jazz's fine releases, there is an excellent selection of Latin, Caribbean, soul-funk jazz and such. Reflecting owner Stuart Baker's eclectic tastes, they also have a superb selection of country and blue-eyed soul albums – perhaps better than anywhere else in London.

In the basement they have music books and used LPs. Upstairs, SOTU has a remarkable stock of new 45s – many are highly collectable tunes that Soul Jazz has licensed and reissued. Thus, I picked up a copy of a 45 I had always wanted to own but never come across: The Wild Magnolias' 'Handa Wanda' (New Orleans Mardi Gras Indian music at its most potent).

Everything here feels right and aimed at a customer base who return time and again. Sounds Of The Universe is beautifully sited in a wide-open building that gets plenty of natural light: it's quite possibly the most ambient record shop in London. Over two decades, this shop, its record label and publishing imprint have achieved remarkable things and show no sign of slowing down. It's not the place to find bargains – 'Handa Wanda' cost me £10! – but no one comes to Soho for cheap thrills these days.

Baker doesn't work behind the counter of SOTU – he's busy overseeing his record label and publishing imprint – and, unlike Richard Branson or Geoff Travis, he shies away from the spotlight. Still, on this occasion he obliged to speak with me.

STUART BAKER

Didn't you first open in Camden Town?

'I was 26 when I opened my first record shop. It was in Camden and was originally called Soul Jazz Records. This is because we Letrasetted the words 'SOUL' and 'JAZZ' onto a bit of white board. The rent was £60 a week and there was one lightbulb, a record player and records (no phone, fax, email, Internet, etc). Later we started a label called Soul Jazz Records and changed the name of the shop to Sounds of the Universe. I counted over twenty other record shops in Camden High Street when we opened. Record shops were everywhere!'

SOTU employee and musician, Anja Ngozi models Soul Jazz LPs.

The SOTU shop is situated in the heart of Soho – did you decide to site it here because of Soho's history of great record shops?

'Yes. I started coming to Soho to buy records when I was 12 or 13 – to buy punk records and also to buy my clothes from Mister Byrite (cheap clothes for kids!). Although we started in Camden High Street, I always knew I wanted to come to Soho.'

The SOTU shop has a very strong musical identity closely allied to the Soul Jazz label. Does the shop primarily exist as an extension of the label or do you see it being an independent entity?

'Hmmm, separate but connected. Hopefully they are related if you know both, and exist on their own and have their own identity if you don't know both.'

The SOTU shop never stocks mainstream pop-rock: does it struggle to survive selling music that's brilliant but niche? I ask as so many other Soho specialist music shops have closed.

'Well, actually we do sell Adele. I walked around Soho one afternoon with my 12-year-old daughter trying to find the records she liked at the time (Adele, Mark Ronson, Ed Sheeran) and could not find them anywhere, so I put in a small 'pop' section as I think 12-year-olds know the future of music. But, yes, we do sell essentially anything non-mainstream (and Soul Jazz Records similarly releases any music that is non-mainstream). It's just what we've always done so I don't really have anything else to compare it with.'

What are your favourite record shops, both historic and contemporary?

'When we were starting out, I wanted to be a mixture of Rough Trade in Covent Garden and Honest Jon's in Portobello Road. I have quite an idyllic memory of the Stiff Records shop – it was the front room of a house in Notting Hill and they only sold Stiff records and Ian Dury, Elvis Costello or The Damned might be hanging out there. I have spent a lot of time in a lot of record shops in America. My favourites are Dr Wax and 2nd Hand Tunes in South Chicago (both closed now), Jazz Record Mart in central Chicago (where Delmark Records comes out of), a Latin store in New York where when I was there the owner was dancing through the aisles of records (like the record store scene in *Rockers* where a guy – I-Roy, I believe – dances across the screen in the store). Bonaparte in Bromley was the first record store I visited (they also had one in Croydon). Long in the Tooth in Philadelphia. Also there was a store called Yanks in Manchester that sold cheap (remaindered) American jazz and soul LPs (like Eddie Harris, Charles Earland, etc.) that I liked a lot. There's a shop/stall in Havana, Cuba, that has a pretty amazing selection of original Cuban music that's been there twenty or so years.'

Above: Music lovers Joisse Clamor and Ella Niles buying records at Sounds Of The Universe. Below: Book section in the basement of Sounds Of The Universe.

Is Record Store Day a good thing? I recall SOTU setting up a sound system and making a big party on Broadwick Street.

'Yes, Record Store Day's proven good for the store and the label and, it appears, the music industry. It got so successful in Soho that I think the council are stopping have sounds systems, etc. outside – shame!'

What is the future of the independent record shop? Is the revival in interest in vinyl and record shops just a fashion or is there a cultural shift under way?

'Well, as I mentioned, I spent quite a period of time in USA buying records and there are more record stores opening every time I go there. Record stores are community spaces – cyphers and meeting points where bands, DJs, collectors, record labels, distributors connect. When everything went digital and many closed, people realised that this was an important role that they played. In USA there are no chain record stores left – only busy independents run for music fans. This is their role!'

RAY'S JAZZ

A stroll east through Soho to Charing Cross Road takes us to the mighty Foyles bookshop. Foyles once had a record department seemingly offering thousands of titles – a large black & white photograph of such when the trade was entirely in 78s is on display by the lifts in the music books section – but this went before the vinyl era. Today, tucked comfortably into a corner on the first floor, sits Ray's Jazz. There's an irony here, considering Ray's started in the basement of Collet's, a now vanished bookshop that sat further down Charing Cross Road from Foyles and, for more than half a century, was its nearest competitor.

Collet's was a 'radical' bookshop (i.e. one affiliated with the British Communist Party at the time) so it likely stocked more Soviet titles than Foyles. In its basement was an excellent record bar specialising in folk and jazz. Ray Smith, who ran the jazz section, was a drummer who swapped his sticks to sell records. Famously grouchy, unflinchingly opinionated and absolutely jazz obsessed, Smith was a Soho habitué and record shop magus. He set up Ray's Jazz on Shaftesbury Avenue in 1974, a shop feted by many (including Charlie Watts, Scott Walker and Henry Rollins) for its deep stock and the staff's encyclopaedic knowledge.

In 2002 Smith announced he would have to close his record shop as they simply couldn't sell enough LPs and CDs to cover the skyrocketing rent. There was an outcry and Foyles stepped in, offering to house the shop in its building. Smith didn't follow his shop – he retired and died not too long after – but Ray's survives, almost two decades on, now managed by gently spoken Dutch national, Frank Van Binsbergen.

I first met Frank when he managed the magnificent jazz section in Tower's Piccadilly shop, so it's fair to say he knows his music. Today, Ray's offers a great selection of new and used LPs and CDs, predominantly jazz but also blues, world, R&B, gospel – just as it always did.

There are also books, magazines (*Jazzwise*, *Downbeat* and such) and a tasty selection of 78s. Actually, the records I most recently purchased here were 78s by Ken Colyer and Count Basie. Thus, I am very happy that Ray's continues. Foyles has the largest selection of music-related books on offer in the UK (plus a huge range of other titles) so it's possible to spend the best part of an afternoon in this magnificent emporium.

Opposite:

Above: Collet's Record Shop advertisement.
Below left: Ray Smith, Ray's Jazz, Foyles. Below right: We buy and sell 78 rpm records.'

AT **Collet's**

Record Shop

180 Shaftesbury Avenue
London WC2H 8JS

Telephone 01 240 3969

A HAPPY CHRISTMAS
TO ALL OUR CUSTOMERS
AND FRIENDS

JAZZ SPECIALISTS FOR THE DISCERNING LISTENER

FROM BUNK TO MONK

FROM GEORGE RUSSELL TO RUSSELL GEORGE
FROM SON HOUSE TO SUN RA
FROM GEORGE LEWIS TO GEORGE LEWIS
FROM HARRY BARRIS TO BARRY HARRIS
FROM BILL PERKINS TO BILL PERKINS
FROM KARL BERGER TO KARL BERGER

TOP SECONDHAND DEPT., ACE MAIL ORDER DEPT., JAPANESE LPs STOCKED.
DISCOUNT SCHEME FOR PERSONAL CALLERS. OPEN MON.-FRI. 10-6 p.m. SAT. 10-4 p.m.

★ ALSO WHILST HERE — VISIT BRITAIN'S BEST INTERNATIONAL FOLK AND BLUES SHOP ★

CAMDEN TOWN

SOUNDS THAT SWING
ROCK 'N' ROLL RESCUE
ALL AGES RECORDS
OUT ON THE FLOOR RECORDS
LET IT ROLL

Camden Town was, pre-pandemic, one of the neighbourhoods that Londoners tended to shy away from, its famous market offering only tourist gridlock. Getting around is difficult enough without having to sidestep Italian couples blocking the pavement while taking selfies or Russian teenagers sulking on the bridge because daddy has refused to buy the entire market for them. As the market now consists largely of T-shirt vendors and fast food outlets there seems little reason to visit.

Yet, once upon a time, the market offered nooks and crannies packed with fascinating traders. Needless to say, in the '90s I would head for the record stalls: there was a Japanese guy who dealt in reggae 45s, an English bloke had suitcases full of vintage – yet mint – Brazilian LPs, a surly white guy called Nick sold an astonishing array of African LPs, while a solidly built young woman (whose hair was an inky, Gorgonish mop) offered up punk and goth records. Sister Ray started as a Camden Market stall, as did Soul Jazz Records. There were plenty of other vinyl vendors, some only occasionally trading, others open whenever I popped by.

By the 1980s Camden competed with Soho and Ladbroke Grove for the title of London's foremost record shop borough: even Tower Records had a branch here (as did Honest Jon's). There were all kinds of collectors' shops and, with its poseurs and punks wanting a pound for a photo and myriad pubs and houseboats and scruffy sense of mischief, Camden exuded London rock 'n' roll's urchin spirit.

Then, when Britpop took off in 1994, Camden overheated with hype and tourists. Inevitably, rents soared, and specialist record shops lost out to those selling tourist/teenage junk; a too-familiar London tale ... Even so, Camden remained – until the pandemic hit – London's foremost live music hub: The Jazz Cafe, The Green Note, The Underworld, Electric Ballroom, Blues Kitchen, Cecil Sharp House, and the aforementioned Dingwalls, are all within a couple of minutes of one another, providing a smorgasbord of concerts by folk, punk, funk, jazz, rock, blues, singer-songwriters and much else. There are also several pubs hosting live music around the high street. The mighty Roundhouse is just past Camden Market in Chalk Farm, while the fabulous Koko, a lush former cinema down towards Mornington Crescent, caught fire in late 2019 and, at time of writing, appears unlikely to reopen as a concert venue.

Oddly, considering the borough's history, Camden didn't become a music hub until the late 1970s. There's little info about Camden record shops of the shellac era. The Cabinet Gramophone Company of 73 Camden

King Rocker Zombie, Camden Town.

Road, founded in 1918/19, manufactured and retailed Fullotone gramophones and accessories (and likely also sold 78s), while A. Selinger at 67 High Street boasted on its 78 sleeves, 'The Brilliant Incandescent and Cycle Accessories Supply Stores' – quite a mouthful, but I get the gist: Camden, being a working-class area, had plenty of bicycle shops and many would have sold 78s alongside cycle accessories (as was de rigueur then).

While it was based in Tottenham rather than Camden, this gives me the opportunity to tell a tale of Hetchin's gramophone store. Hyman Hetchin (1894–1961) opened his gramophone shop on Seven Sisters Road in 1922. Like many dealers in the early days, he also sold bicycles. In 1934, he went into partnership with Jack Denny (1906–91) to manufacture racing bicycles of Denny's design. These became so successful that the music side of the business was discontinued. As a devoted cyclist, I love

the idea of a combined bicycle/record shop: perhaps it's time for someone to open one? Tottenham is certainly short of both …

Back in the late 1960s Blue Horizon, the blues label that launched Peter Green's Fleetwood Mac, ran a small record shop out of their Mornington Crescent building. Both shop and label closed by 1971, leaving Kay's Irish Music Centre, situated next to the Catholic church on Arlington Road, as Camden's only record shop. Kay's sold records from Irish entertainers alongside Elvis Presley and Jim Reeves (both honorary Irish icons).

Hard as it is to now imagine, Camden was once Irish London's epicentre – there's a scene in the movie *Withnail & I* where the two main characters, both 'resting' actors and fops, to boot (it's 1969), enter a local Irish pub and find themselves unwelcome – and it was these people desiring music from 'back home' that Kay's served. The Pogues, who had strong Irish Camden connections, were apparently loyal customers.

The Pogues were also loyal customers at Camden's greatest-ever record shop, Rock On. As with Kay's, Rock On no longer exists but, for almost two decades, it was the UK's foremost record shop for rockabilly, R&B, Cajun, zydeco, garage bands and more, much more!

Rock On began with Ted Carroll opening a Ladbroke Grove market stall in 1972, so I'll tell the story of the stall's rise in the West London chapter. His success there (and in Soho Market) led to the setting up of Ace Records, a label devoted to reissuing rare records that customers asked for but were near impossible to find. Wanda Jackson, James Carr, Link Wray and Barbara Lynn (among many others) found new audiences via Ace's reissues. Ace also recorded some of the new bands who were then shaking up London town, most notably Motorhead. Needing a record shop out of

Right: *Rock On advertisement.*

Below: *Vicki Fox working at Rock On record shop circa 1978. (Courtesy of ACE Records)*

Funky films and music at Honest Jon's.

Uneasy listening.

which to run Ace, Carroll chose to do so in seedy, rundown, Irish Camden Town.

Rock On's record shop opened right by Camden Town tube station in late 1975. It was the right place at the right time – Camden had Dingwalls, a music venue booking the kind of bands that loved Rock On, alongside old Irish ballrooms then being transformed into music spaces. Camden Market was, back then, a place where all kinds of energies got under way, while The Roundhouse, a noted rock concert venue since the late 1960s, would soon feature concerts by The Ramones, Flamin' Groovies and other US bands who represented a new sound and spirit in rock; a sound and spirit that Rock On's stock encapsulated and the aforementioned bands, and many others, would become customers. Local lads Madness were regulars and, for their 1981 film *Take It Or Leave It*, would shoot a scene in Rock On.

Rock On's success encouraged others to open record shops in Camden and, by the late 1980s, there were dozens of shops and stalls both in and around the high street and market. The rise in media interest in Camden ensured the market boomed and reports that Britpop's stars might all be found holding court (separately) ensured teenagers, wannabes, groupies, drug dealers, bullshit artists and visiting tourists flocked here as an earlier generation once did to Carnaby Street. When Amy Winehouse signed her record deal, she used her advance to purchase an apartment in Camden. Did she go record shopping here? Well, of course.

Inevitably, rents were hiked and by the mid-1990s, Rock On's era as Camden Town's premiere vintage vinyl dealers was coming to an end. Having built Ace Records into the world's leading reissue label for rockabilly and soul recordings, Carroll and his business partners and staff settled happily into a Harlesden industrial estate. Many of the other Camden record shops had less happy endings, rent hikes forcing them to close.

SOUNDS THAT SWING

Today, a handful of record shops remain. All survived the pandemic and continue to represent Camden's raucous spirit. On Parkway sits Sounds That Swing. This small but perfectly formed shop channels Rock On's spirit, dealing as it does in vintage rockabilly, blues, R&B, garage bands and such. Some of the stock is used but there's plenty of new releases, largely vinyl LPs and 45s, but also a decent selection of CDs (the likes of Ace Records still focus on excellent CD compilations). Stepping into Sounds That Swing, you feel like you've been teleported back to 1950s USA, the shop's sound and vision suggesting an era when Elvis was slim and segregation legal.

Unlike the myriad diners who attempt to recreate a 1950s décor and, inevitably, make everything dull and bloodless, Sounds That Swing is lively, offbeat, a retro Americana hangout full of wild sounds and obscure records. That the late DJ and record producer Andrew Weatherall was a regular customer here is, to my mind, unsurprising.

Co-owners Martin Heaphy and Neil Scott are friendly men who have spent good chunks of their adult lives on the rockin' circuit, so certainly know the music they deal in well. Both are also a pleasure to chat with, always offering tips on offbeat records I've never heard of and putting aside 45s that tickle my fancy. They also run the No Hit Records label that reissues impossibly rare music of the kind that Sounds That Swing specialises in. If you want rarities by Link Wray or Johnny 'Guitar' Watson – I've found both here – this is the place to head. Down in the basement – and only open at weekends – was Vinyl Boutique, a used rock LP shop run by Boz Boorer, a guitarist whose day job is leading Morrissey's band (ponder on just what this might involve). Lockdown meant Boz decided not to reopen.

Sounds That Swing opened on nearby Inverness Street in 1995 and relocated to Parkway in 2009. Originally founded by Barney Koumis, in 2016 he sold the shop to its manager, Neil Scott with Martin Heaphy coming in full time. Neil & Martin know one another so well that when one of them begins to answer one of my questions, the other will quite often finish it.

NEIL SCOTT & MARTIN HEAPHY

'We were on Inverness Street by Alan Bennett's house from 1995 and stayed there for fifteen years,' says Neil. 'It was an odd location as there were no other shops about so no passing foot traffic – except for when they put cameras in the bottom of Inverness Street, so all the drug dealers graduated up to where we were based!

Sounds That Swing's owner, Neil Scott.

Below: Nick Martin models Elvis LP.

It was a shack. Falling apart. Leaking when it rained. You could hear the rats running about in the ceiling. But we did have great records. Because we were very niche – specialising in rockabilly and R&B and garage and a bit of punk and lounge and country and such – we quickly found customers. We opened around the same time as Rock On was closing and, while Camden was full of record shops, no one was doing what Rock On did. So we were like a continuation and this worked well for us. Rock On was a genius record shop.'

'I'd known Neil and Barney for a long time,' says Martin, 'and I was lending Barney vintage paperback books for the covers of a series of LPs he was issuing called *Desperate Rock & Roll*. Back then I was working a dull day job but very much part of the rocking scene – DJ'ing, buying and selling records, going to all the concerts and weekends – so getting a job here was a way of me making it full time.'

'During the '90s the CD was dominant and, although we were a specialist record shop, we did (and do) stock a lot of CDs,' says Neil. 'The shop revolves round the rock 'n' roll 45 and we've shaped it for that. Stock is 50/50 new and used. There are so many new reissues these days – more than ever before. And old American stuff is not so easy to find these days – but we go out and look for it. A lot of collectors are getting old and selling their collections. Or dying.

'We also ensure we visit America every year. When we are there, we hit all the shops we know of and the record fairs. With the Internet there are less bargains to be found but you can still find good stuff. The thing about collecting old records is that a record we don't rate can mean something completely different to someone else – and vice versa.'

'Sometimes you have to live with a record for a few months and then it grows on you,' adds Martin, before adding, 'other times it remains awful and you just want to get rid of it! But someone else might think it's a classic.'

'We have sold records that are worth £5,000,' says Neil. 'Not often, admittedly. But we do regularly have 45s worth £200 – £300 – £400.'

'The thing about collecting records is too many people treat it as list ticking – they just want to own what they have been told are the essential records,' says Neil. 'But what's needed is explorers, people who will go out and buy obscure records and listen to them and then share their enthusiasm when they come across lost treasure. That's how the music gets shared. And that's one of our shop's guiding principles – to get all kinds of good music out there, not just the stuff you already know. And to do this we have to buy loads of rubbish and listen through it until we get to something tasty.'

'Being in Camden means we get all kinds of people dropping in,' notes Martin. 'From tourists who wander about not even knowing what a record shop is – after ten minutes they finally approach the counter and ask in a baffled voice what is it we sell! – to loyal customers, to kids who turn up with amazing knowledge and great taste. It's incredibly varied. We have customers who are famous rock stars and actors, and we treat them with the same courtesy that we treat everyone else. That there are very few record shops trading in rockabilly and R&B means we have an international reputation, so we do get collectors from all over the world visiting.'

'Dedication and stupidity!' is Neil's answer to my question on how Sounds That Swing has survived. 'It's a vocation – not as important as being a doctor or a nurse but I do feel that running a specialist record shop means engaging with people in a positive way. You don't make much money doing a shop like this but if you love the music then you feel happy about going to work each day.'

As for Camden Town's future, Neil and Martin have mixed feelings. 'The market has changed so much. People used to be able to go in there and sell tat. Not any more,' says Martin. 'But that's London, everywhere has changed. What we do have now is a return of record shops to Camden and this is a good thing. It attracts foot traffic, people come here to shop for records. And we're all friendly – if someone comes in wanting new punk, we can send them to All Ages. Reggae to Out On The Floor. And vice versa.'

In Rock 'N' Roll Rescue you ccn find used records, instruments, stereo gear, books, memorabilia, clothes and shoes.

ROCK 'N' ROLL RESCUE

A few doors up on Parkway is Rock 'N' Roll Rescue, next door to The Dublin Castle (where Madness made their mark and tens of thousands of aspiring young bands have strode the stage). It is a charity shop specialising in, as its name suggests, anything to do with rock. So you can find instruments, amplifiers, books, magazines, memorabilia, clothes and more here. But its main trade is in used records and, somehow, they constantly get good stock in. What kind of stock? Oh, all kinds of things, but as I'm always happy to buy old American 45s I must admit they do seem to source such – Tommy James & the Shondells' 'Hanky Panky' and a Roy Byrd 45 are just two of the gems I've sourced here.

Rock 'N' Roll Rescue was founded – and continues to be run by – Knox, the musician best known as leader of The Vibrators, one of the first London punk bands. Being a charity (staff are volunteers) and having punk connections means, on occasion, I've found the most striking shop assistants behind the counter: Mohawks, tattooed faces, the whole Mad Max shebang. You know what? The service is always friendly.

The music charity shop Rock 'N' Roll Rescue beside the music venue, The Dublin Castle, on Parkway.

ALL AGES RECORDS

Speaking of punk leads us to All Ages Records, a record shop on Pratt Street that specialises in punk rock/hardcore (what, you ask, is the difference? Hardcore is, I think it's fair to say, unremittingly fast and punishing). Alongside Brighton's Punker Bunker, All Ages Records is the only UK record shop to keep the punk flag flying. Considering the likes of Rough Trade and Small Wonder both made their marks as punk rock shops, this is an honourable calling.

Owner Nick Collins opened All Ages Records in 2003, managing to remain in business without ever having to compromise his vision of selling punk-thrash-hardcore alongside the myriad genres now associated (2-Tone-mod-death metal, etc.), plus fanzines (a punk tradition that, like the genre, has made a comeback recently), badges, stickers, mugs, gig tickets, books and a wide selection of punk T-shirts.

While some might think punk died with Sid Vicious – or John Lydon's increasingly infantile behaviour – the music retains a loyal following and visiting punk fans are now far more likely to make a pilgrimage to Camden Town (after all, The Clash did rehearse here) than stroll down the King's Road (as once was the case). Indeed, the last of London's punk Mohican tribe are known to hang out on the bridge before the market, posing for all and sundry while cadging a few quid off the tourists who want to photograph them. Appropriate, then, that All Ages Records is based here.

Collins smiles broadly when I ask how international his client base is, noting that All Ages attracts customers from across the globe. The records and CDs his shop sells reflect this, demonstrating how punk's status as a protest music continues in many nations. Nick's an enthusiastic chap, who loves to talk about new and old punk records – one of his perennial favourites (and a solid seller) is *Fresh Fruit for Rotting Vegetables*, the Dead Kennedys' debut LP. Anarcho UK punk band The Subhumans also receive his keen support.

Nick Collins, owner of All Ages Records, with Yellow.

Digging for records at All Ages Records, Camden.

All Ages is something of a magnet for punk musicians across the globe and many want their records to be stocked here, thus, sorting through the huge selection of LPs, 45s, CDs and tapes on offer can be a challenge: I've never heard of most of the bands, so where would I start? Collins encourages bands to drop their gig flyers and other such stuff to ensure his shop can help promote what is, these days, a very underground scene. He didn't mention a 'punk community' but All Ages Records really does exist to serve this.

Being a movie buff ensures that Collins has turned the back room of All Ages into a space stocked with cult movie DVDs – just ask politely and you will be allowed entry into this sanctuary. A punk rock record shop combined with a cult video shop is extremely niche and quite brilliant. I should note that Nick doesn't have a Mohawk or wear safety pins. Actually, he doesn't look anything like the punks who help out at Rock 'N' Roll Rescue. Which is fine, running All Ages is a very punk rock thing to do.

Having two fluffy dogs – Bob and Yellow – to keep him company marks Collins out as a gentle chap. And he is. He may love spikey, aggressive music but All Ages is non-confrontational. It's also, obviously, the love of his life: he speaks eloquently of how awful lockdown was because all he wanted to do was be in his shop, playing records to people and proselytising about punk. Instead, he was stuck at home going stir crazy. Now that Collins is trading again, All Ages is open every day – including bank/public holidays. For those still loyal to punk, All Ages serves as its London temple.

Out On The Floor Records, Inverness Street, Camden Town.

OUT ON THE FLOOR RECORDS

Out On The Floor Records has been trading in Camden for thirty plus years – yes, it now is Camden's oldest record shop – with owners Jake Travis and Mick Marshall having run the shop for the last two decades. They're an affable pair and ensure Out On The Floor provides new and used LPs and 45s you are unlikely to find in the other Camden record shops. Thus, there's lots of rock and soul and jazz and reggae, Jake being owner of Tuff Scout, a label issuing new reggae recordings in very distinctive sleeves. Ask to see the box of rare ska and rocksteady 45s Jake keeps behind the counter and stare in awe at these wonders from simpler times. Then realise they are priced at today's eBay rates ...

Being on Inverness Street, a pedestrianised street colonised by an overflow of market traders, means Out On The Floor is sometimes overlooked, but this is a mistake as it's an engaging place to dig. What did I last purchase here? Johnny Taylor's *Taylored Silk* LP plus 45s by Joe Tex, Thin Lizzy, Clarence Carter and Lloyd Price.

JAKE TRAVIS

'Out On The Floor opened way before my time,' says Jake. 'Mick took the shop over on 1 January 2000 with Finn. I came in 2003, buying Finn out. I was initially a customer of Finn's, buying reggae, but Mick had also provided me with some stock when I was very briefly doing a stall in Brick Lane. We are in central Camden but not quite on the main drag, hence slightly cheaper rent but still a good deal of passing footfall; someone told me Camden is London's second biggest tourist attraction next to Buckingham Palace! We sell pretty much across the board with lots of reggae, both cheap and collectable. So we appeal to people just wanting a Clash or Amy Winehouse record and those who want to come in and have a proper dig. We've always had a turntable for the public so they can play stuff.

'Starting Tuff Scout ten years ago has, without doubt, been a highlight of my time at the shop. With Gil Cang, we have been fortunate to record Big Youth, Michael Prophet, Papa Levi and many more great talents. We've also recorded non-reggae singers: Lou Rhodes from Lamb and the great Carleen Anderson. Our *Inna London Dub* LP has sold really well, and we are just about to release its follow-up: a dedication to all reggae shops, new and old, titled modestly *Out On The Floor Dub*.

'Throughout the '90s, CDs were a big part of the business and, even when I arrived, the whole right-hand side was CDs. Then demand fell off and now we only stock a selection of reggae CDs. Things were very lean for a while: we survived because of our location and the reggae faithful. Things have improved in the last few years due to the vinyl revival.

'Our customer demographic has changed from predominantly middle-aged men to a younger, mixed crowd, which is great. But don't believe the hype – vinyl has gone from flatlining to now a blip on music sales. The vast percentage of public get their music online. That said, we are niche, and niche is often able to survive when other businesses go down.'

OOTF's Jay 'Who Cork The Dance' models Tuff Scout's *Ruff And Tuff* LP.

Let the music play. Artwork on the wall by @vanemg.art.

Andres Puentes sits outside Let It Roll Records on Kentish Town Road.

LET IT ROLL

Back on my bike, I cycled towards Let It Roll Records, 121 Kentish Town Road. One of my pedals snapped off on the way there, ensuring I'd later have a very slow journey back to South London. Let It Roll is the Camden baby, opening in 2017, of hard-rock-loving Dubliner, Kieran Smyth. Sited a short distance from Camden Town, Let It Roll is spacious and stocks new and used LPs and 45s.

Upon entering you immediately encounter Café Pepita, vendors of delicious Colombian coffee. Andres and Melissa Puentes run the café alongside overseeing Let It Roll while Kieran works on documentaries. Grungy Kentish Town Road thus offers superb coffee and great vinyl all in one shop: here I found Johnny Thunders' *So Alone* LP and Puncture's 'Mucky Pup' 45 (a holy grail for this collector). Let It Roll's spaciousness and back garden means, once the pandemic is over, it can again be used for DJ parties and much else.

As the pandemic is likely to force great changes on a neighbourhood that has long been dependent on tourism, Camden's raffish spirit might just thrive again. Or it could continue as a crock of crap. Either way, I hope its record shops survive.

THE DAMNED
TERROR
LIVE BY THE CODE
ADOLESCENTS
RAMONES
HEY HO LET'S GO
DAMNED
Closed Casket
Damned
bad brains
HEY HO LET'S GO RAMONES
TOMMY JOHNNY JOEY DEEDEE
THE DAMNED
MISFITS
MEAT FREE PERSON
VEGGIE PUNK
BLACK FLAG
deathwish
CHAOS
YOUNG BLOOD
UMLAUT RECORDS
WORLD BE FREE
THE ANTI-CIRCLE
POWER TRIP
TAANG! RECORDS
MISFITS
DAMNED
BRIDGE NINE
RUN FOR COVER
R F C
PUNKS NOT DEAD

muzique tropique
collection
selected material from the
muzique tropique catalogue remixed by...
glasgow
Technics

LADBROKE GROVE

HONEST JON'S

ROUGH TRADE WEST

PEOPLE'S SOUND RECORDS

Russian oligarchs, bankers and the landed gentry – it's easy to get an impression of the aforementioned demographic now occupying all of West London. In fact, the area remains a patchwork of neighbourhoods that vary greatly, some exclusive, others much less so. The Grenfell Tower tragedy highlighted how a working-class, minority community can exist only minutes from Holland Park's elite.

Shepherd's Bush is home to Pecking's Studio One (81 Askew Rd, London W12 9AH), a shop that has been selling fresh Jamaican records since 1973, its founder, George Price, having started distributing JA music in London in the early 1960s. Notting Hill Gate, once a hippie Mecca, was where Virgin had their headquarters: 'Want lentils with your Yes triple LP, man?' That's long gone, the Notting Hill shops are now home only to the mothership of Record & Tape Exchange (R&TE), the UK's largest used record/CD/DVD shop. R&TE never generates much love from customers – surly staff, high prices, poor exchange – but it handles so much stock that you can find interesting items here (and in its gentler Greenwich branch). A twenty-minute stroll (or ten-minute cycle) down the Portobello Road takes you to Ladbroke Grove, one of those neighbourhoods where London's cosmopolitan soul continues to strut its funky stuff.

Ladbroke Grove has a street market, antique shops, plentiful ethnic eateries and two of the world's foremost record shops. I've not come across a great deal of information regarding pre-Second World War record shops in this area: J.B. Cramer & Co., noted British piano manufacturers and gramophone retailers, had a department store at 136 Notting Hill Gate, while Hope Norman & Co. were based at 85 Westbourne Grove.

G. Littlewood, 'Gramophone & Cycle Dealer' stood at 268 Portobello Road (now where the Westway stands, thus no trace of Littlewood's remains beyond a sense of historic energies emanating from a spot situated in between the Grove's current triangle of record shops). Littlewood's 78 sleeves carry the printed instruction, 'Under no consideration can this Record be exchanged', yet, beyond the text on 78 sleeves almost nothing is left to document these shops. I think it's fair to surmise that it wasn't until the 1950s that this area – ironically then seen as one of London's poorest – first came into its own as a music hub.

For much of the second half of the twentieth century, Ladbroke Grove was where London's alternative energies gathered. Full of dilapidated housing owned by slum landlords, the Grove had a rough reputation – the 1958 'race riots' were sparked by racist Teddy Boys

Pianist Diz Watson and band stopping traffic outside Rock On, 93 Golborne Road, 1982. (Photo by Brian Neville, courtesy of ACE Records)

attacking West Indian locals (Oswald Mosley's Fascist Union Movement regularly rabble roused here), while, in 1976, Notting Hill Carnival saw Black youths battling the police. Negative headlines ensured this pocket of West London attracted little investment and, in its isolation, everything from Notting Hill Carnival through crusty hippie space rockers Hawkwind, to Release, the first organisation to provide help for individuals arrested on drugs charges, took shape in the district. Alongside sizeable West Indian, working-class English, and Romany Gypsy communities, many beatniks, hippies, punks, political radicals and hustlers/entrepreneurs/misfits all found the Grove a suitably sympathetic environment to settle.

Inevitably, a counterculture of sorts evolved here, ensuring several spectacularly good record shops opened – from calypso and jazz through soul and psychedelic rock to punk and dub – while Portobello Road Market offered plenty of stalls selling new and used music. The Grove's community spirit made it an exciting neighbourhood and, even today, with gentrification having transformed much of Notting Hill into a playground for the extremely wealthy, wandering along Portobello Road, under the Westway and into Golborne Road remains a pleasure. A pleasure that offers plenty of delights for crate diggers.

Post-Second World War, the first music vendor of note in Ladbroke Grove appears to have been The Calypso Shop. Opened on the corner of Portobello Road and Blenheim Crescent by brothers Michael and David Tobin, The Calypso Shop might be the first UK record shop owned by Black Britons.

Calypso, the witty Trinidadian speak-song style, had been developing across the first half of the twentieth century but took off internationally after the Second World War – US troops stationed in Trinidad had picked up on this Afro-Caribbean music and so helped to make Lord Invader's 'Rum & Coca-Cola' a huge hit when covered by The Andrew Sisters. Several calypsonians settled in the UK, none more celebrated than Lord Kitchener, who arrived on the *Empire Windrush* and scored with 'London is the Place for Me'. There's not much information available about The Calypso Shop, but it is known to have provided a base for local activists during the 1958 Notting Hill race riots and could be considered as both London's first Black music specialist *and* front-line record shop.

By 1962 Chris Blackwell, the young Anglo-Jamaican founder of Island Records, was setting up in London. Music contacts led him to Lee Gopthal, an Indian Jamaican who would initially serve as his landlord. Blackwell helped finance his fledgling record label by selling new Jamaican 45s from a stall on Portobello Road and Gopthal, seeing the money that could be made from Jamaican music, set up as a distributor. With British record shops oblivious to or unwelcoming towards the new Kingston sounds, Gopthal opened his own record shops.

Musicland record shop at 230 Portobello Road opened in 1966 and Gopthal would go on to open Musicland record shops across London – some doing well, others lasting only a matter of months. Alongside Musicland, he also opened the Muzik City chain, focusing on

Jamaican and African American music. These employed Black staff (then a rare occurrence on the UK high street).

The Ladbroke Grove Musicland proved a hit, it having deep album stock, so lots of jazz and R&B – which appealed to both the West Indians and bohemians – and rock, which was what the hippies wanted. Notting Hill had many squats, and the area around Ladbroke Grove was hippie central in the late 1960s. Hippie hard rockers' Hawkwind and Free lived around here and *Performance*, the Mick Jagger movie about a gangster hiding out in a reclusive rock singer's scuzzy apartment, was filmed in Powis Square. How Gopthal, who never claimed to have any great passion for music, got things so right is unknown (he died in 1989), but he employed good shop managers and Musicland gained a reputation as the foremost outlet for imported psychedelic rock albums.

While Musicland was selling new rock albums, Rock On specialised in selling old rock 'n' roll 45s. I mentioned Rock On in the Camden Town section, but it was as a stall in the covered flea market at 93 Golborne Road that Ted Carroll first started trading in August 1971. And by doing so, he pioneered the rise of vintage vinyl shops (plus lots more).

Ted Carroll, an Irish record collector and band manager, decided to rent a stall to shift some of the vintage 45s he had accumulated while working as US tour manager for the Irish rock band Skid Row. Initially, Carroll only opened on Saturdays – the rest of the week he was busy managing a young Dublin band called Thin Lizzy – but Rock On immediately proved a hit. Back then, it was very difficult to find old records by artists who weren't superstars, the labels often deleting singles when their chart run was over.

Carroll had picked up a great number of rare R&B and rockabilly 45s while in Boston. A sojourn in Dublin led to an attic full of mint condition 45s by the likes of Ike & Tina Turner and The Ronettes on the London label. Being a collector (but not a hoarder) meant Carroll decided to unload his excess 45s and it was these he initially stocked Rock On with.

Think about it: back then there were almost no reissues – beyond a handful of LPs compiling early jazz and blues recordings – and few got to travel to the USA in search of musical treasures. Second-hand record shops and stalls existed but, more often than not, these were junk emporiums. Rock On changed all this and, almost immediately, its reputation ensured Carroll would find customers queuing outside for him to open.

Among those customers were Jimmy Page, Lemmy and, of course, the Irish Casanova, Phil Lynott. The latter loved to hang out at Rock On and listen to oldies but goodies. So much so, he wrote 'The Rocker', a song where he sings, 'I get my records at the Rock On stall/sweet rock and roll/Teddy boy, he's got them all'.

Rock On's success determined that Carroll opened a branch in Soho Market (a space long since demolished). The Soho Rock On, managed by fellow Irish music biz veteran Roger Armstrong, was open Tuesday–Saturday and did a roaring trade, with John Peel and Charlie Gillett (among other BBC DJs) becoming regulars.

The Soho and Ladbroke Grove Rock Ons became hubs for the musicians who would go on to form the first wave of London punk bands: Joe Strummer purchased 'Brand New Cadillac' there; Malcolm McLaren came, with Steve Jones and Paul Cook in tow, searching for material for his King's Road shop jukebox and for the fledgling Sex Pistols to cover; while Paul Weller purchased 45s by Small Faces and other '60s artists that held his ear. (When The Jam were starting out, they turned up in Soho Market wanting to play an impromptu set and Armstrong plugged them into Rock On's power supply. The Camden Town chapter details their magnificent emporium there.)

Also operating on Golborne Road, back then, was one of the first Record & Tape Exchange outlets – in the 1990s this chain of used record shops appeared to be everywhere (today, only the Notting Hill Gate and Greenwich branches continue to trade). Opening nearby, at 76 Golborne Road in 1973, was All Change Records, a used record shop run by Geoff Francis and Graham Griffith. Immediately successful, the duo went on to open a small chain of record shops, selling new and used records (with Griffith emphasising his passion for jazz). In 1974 they passed the Golborne Road shop on to two employees, Jon Clare and Dave Ryner. The shop was renamed Honest Jon's – Clare is just such a Jon – and would develop into a remarkable emporium, especially when it shifted to 278 Portobello Road (owned by employees Mark Ainley and Alan Scholefield since 1992).

Shan Tilakumara brought his children, Anuk and Sabini, to Honest Jon's.

HONEST JON'S

Honest Jon's has achieved remarkable things over its near half a century of trading. It has expanded into Chelsea, Covent Garden, Camden and Soho (and subsequently retreated from all), most recently opening an outlet in the Coal Drops Yard (King's Cross). The Honest Jon's record label has issued music from across the globe – including the brilliant *London is the Place for Me* series of compilations that take the wry Lord Kitchener anthem as a starting point to look at Black music-making in London from the dawn of the recorded era up until the 1960s.

Many notable figures have worked behind the counter – the founders of the World Circuit, Blood & Fire and Mo' Wax record labels all pulled shifts – and its clientele is legendary. Today, Honest Jon's remains a small shop that is crammed with vinyl (and CDs), largely new, focusing on jazz-soul-reggae–outernational (African-Caribbean-Asian-Latin and beyond) and much else. It's eclectic and electric and a fascinating place to find the records you want alongside those you never knew existed (but should do).

ALAN SCHOLEFIELD

How was business during lockdown?

'Incredibly busy. Normally we are 6–8 guys working as a team in the shop, mail order and the record label and we had to furlough the staff and put the label under wraps. I came into the shop on the first Monday after lockdown and looked on the computer and saw that mail order was starting to get busy. I thought, 'Well, I should handle these orders', and that's what I've done for the last two months. There's been a groundswell of incredible love and loyalty from customers across the world – and not just to us but to all kinds of independent businesses. Mail order has been incredibly busy – after a while, I had to get one of the staff in to help with the orders. I think it's a truism to say that lockdown was easier than reopening – which is a real challenge. "What measures do we need in place for social distancing?", "Can we touch the records without gloves on?" It's a problem, a funny one. I think there's a story to tell at the end of it all.'

Honest Jon's co-owner Alan Schloefield.

Honest Jon's is the longest-serving Ladbroke Grove record shop. Why do you think it's survived when many others have folded?

'A bit of luck and serendipity and God smiled on us. Honest Jon's has always had interesting people working for it. When Jon Clare employed us, he thought Mark and I were interesting people. And the shop has embraced these specialised areas with love and knowledge. There's a really loyal constituency out there of people who love things like free jazz. Now, there's not a huge number of them, but there's very few record shops that stock the kind of stuff like free jazz or releases on obscure independent labels from across the world, so people have always headed to us for such. My business partner, Mark Ainley, is an exceptional record man – he's quite a unique guy. Also, it's a good area for music. The Windrush generation Afro-Caribbean community who settled here gave the Grove an incredible character. And the English, when they get into something, they really get into it – whether its blues in the '60s or reggae in the '70s or dance music, or whatever – so this really supports a shop like Honest Jon's. So it's partly geography, partly psycho-geography, the interesting people who gather around such a shop ... all of it.'

Are you surprised by the revival of record shops in recent years?

'I started here in 1988 and I think Mark and I took over the shop from Jon in '92, so yes, we've seen every kind of change in the record trade imaginable. We started off with Mark going to the USA and bringing back suitcases full of amazing records and that was a really good base to build on. We initially ignored the digital revolution and then it really hit us around the turn of the century, with sales dropping across the board, and we realised "this is a major cultural change".

'We had to adapt to survive, and we did this by working with lots of independent labels from across the globe and setting up our own Honest Jon's label. So we became a shop you came to because it was likely no one else in London was stocking much of what we had. When Tower closed – and they had such a huge selection of specialist music – it left the field open to us and, say, Soul Jazz, for a lot of records most shops would never consider stocking. That meant you had to come to us if you wanted to find such releases.

'What's been happening in recent years is this fetishisation of vinyl records – either towards super-expensive vinyl pressings or overpricing used records. I'm not keen on either. We've never been vinyl fetishists. Yes, we all go home and worship our vinyl altars [laughs], but I've always been happy to stock

Interior of Honest Jon's.

and own CDs and find them often just as good as a vinyl release and far more functional: you don't have to get up and turn them over and they take up a lot less space!

'The vast majority of our stock is new, but we occasionally buy collections in – often from the estate of a long-time customer, so that sometimes provides an interesting selection. We even have several boxes of 78s in the basement! But the days of going to Omaha and finding crates full of unsold Blue Note LPs is long gone. So we don't really try and compete with used record shops.'

How's the Honest Jon's record label been doing? What are the forthcoming releases on the label?

'The label has been a natural outgrowth of the record shop. I'm a fan of record shop record labels and love to hear about the different ones that have existed over the years. Something like *London is the Place for Me* has been a great calling card for the shop. When we started out, we were with EMI and we did a collection of Candi Staton's Muscle Shoals recordings that sold over 100,000 copies. So some of our releases have been very successful while others possess more niche appeal. We're about to release *A Stranger I May Be*, a series of albums documenting Savoy's gospel recordings as a three CD set and three double vinyl albums.

'The label's been a label of love – it buttressed us at a time when the world was changing and gave us a business model and I'm very happy it continues to exist. We've never made a fortune running Honest Jon's but I'm very proud of what we've achieved.'

Any thoughts on the future of London record retail?

'London rents have become astronomical in recent years, just ridiculous. And this has been extremely detrimental to businesses such as ours. If anything good comes out of the pandemic it would be a levelling of the rents, allowing small businesses to breathe again.'

Rough Trade West record shop in Notting Hill, London.

ROUGH TRADE WEST

Only six minutes' stroll away from Honest Jon's is Rough Trade West at 130 Talbot Road. Opened by Geoff Travis at 202 Kensington Park Road in summer 1976, Rough Trade was, initially, a base for Travis to unload large numbers of LPs he had purchased very cheaply while travelling in the USA. He also stocked new music coming from New York City, Kingston, Dusseldorf and beyond.

Fortuitously, when punk exploded across London later that year, Rough Trade turned out to be among the first record shops to serve as a hub for the new music. Travis then launched Rough Trade's eponymous record label and distribution service, ensuring his Ladbroke Grove record shop served as punk's epicentre. Those were wild days with skinheads attacking customers and yardies robbing the shop of its takings at gun point, reflecting the Grove when it was rough and ready.

You need to read *Going for a Song* if you want to learn of Travis's journey from record shop owner to record label magnet but, I should note, he sold the shop and its stock to three staff members in 1982. Due to their landlord having little faith, they promptly shifted across the Portobello Road to Talbot Road (and continue to trade here). Today, Rough Trade West remains a remarkable record shop, its walls still covered in posters from that halcyon era when punk shook London. It has largely new stock – the basement holds used – with a focus on all kinds of alternative music (rock, electronic, dance, folk). In-store performances by notable artists have been held here – the superb Irish psyche-folk band Lankum raised the roof on a wet winter night in late 2019 – and hopefully, post-pandemic, will do so again. These events ensure the energies that once sparked through the original shop continue to inspire music fans.

Nigel House was one of the trio that Travis sold the Rough Trade shop to and he now manages all of the Rough Trade shops.

NIGEL HOUSE

'I started at Rough Trade in 1981 or '82. I still don't know what was going on then, with the Rough Trade organisation. There was the label and the distribution network, and all kinds of problems, and the accountants were called in and they said, "Close the shop, it's losing money" but I'm sure we weren't losing money – you know accountants, they can prove anything they want. So we three staff (Nigel, Pete, Jude) bought the stock of the shop off Geoff [Travis]. It was very touch and go because we had to go to the bank and get a loan to do so and what we were offering as collateral was the very stock we were borrowing the money to buy!

'At the same time, the landlord of the original shop wanted us out. He didn't trust us to survive so we had to shift from Kensington Park Road around the corner to Talbot Road, where the Rough Trade West shop remains. We took a lot of the posters and record sleeves that were on the wall of the original shop to Talbot Road and, over the years, have continued to layer more material over them so when we had to soundproof the ceiling a few years ago we found these remarkable posters from the dawn of the shop – a Sex Pistols Anarchy tour, a Clash Futura 2000 poster – that had been buried for years!

'We set up with the three of us on a tiny wage – we paid ourselves the equivalent of the dole – and initially scraped by, as we had gone from employees to owners so were having to pay all the expenses. By then, 1982, the shop had calmed down a lot. We weren't getting the Ladbroke Grove skinheads coming in and causing havoc, so the security guard – who shifted with us from the old shop – wasn't needed any more.

'I don't want to say that those days were better than today, but they were incredibly exciting times to be working at Rough Trade. We'd get these boxes of American hardcore records in – the Bad Brains, Black Flag – and no one had ever heard rock music like that before. I remember breaking open one box and it contained Husker Du's "8 Miles High" and selling it straight out of the box to a customer.

'That said, there has never been a boom period for Rough Trade. We never set up as a chart shop so didn't sell loads of Oasis or Blur CDs during the Britpop boom. At the same time, the supermarkets selling chart CDs didn't hit us like they did a lot of shops. The challenge today, with running a record shop like Rough Trade, is to still be able to source new records that are subversive and fun. Many musicians now are so reluctant to say anything that might upset someone or mark them out as political. Back then, music certainly had an edge to it.

'Rough Trade is a cultural hub. Music's not separate from the rest of culture – maybe it's too available – the way you can just press a button and have it on your computer. That detracts from the pleasure of digging for a record. I certainly believe there is more excitement in coming to a record shop and getting your music than buying on line.'

Al Mills has worked at Rough Trade West for four years.

SATURDAY 16th SEPTEMBER at 4·00
10% OFF
NEW RELEASES
NEW RELEASES
NEW RELEASE I
NEW RELEASE T.
NEW RELEASE F.
NEW RELEASE S.
FRAZEY FORD
U KIN B THE SUN
Selected reissues from Gilles Peterson's Basement Archive.
Shining light on magnificent records and the stories that brought them to us.
NEW RELEASE. B
NEW RELEASE M.
Bell X1
NEW RELEASE. A.

PEOPLE'S SOUND RECORDS

A couple of minutes' walk from Rough Trade takes you to People's Sound Records at 11 All Saints Road. Opening in the 1980s, People's Sound Records is the last reggae shop standing in the Grove. This reflects on how the neighbourhood has changed in the past twenty years – Notting Hill still hosts Carnival every August, but the West Indian community are now far less prominent. Indeed, All Saints Road, once thought of as 'the front line' – reggae, marijuana and rice and peas were all staples here – is now an upmarket street where Tory MPs settle. Thus, People's Sound stands out, both as a proud emblem of the West Indian community who gave this area such character, and as a relic (of sorts) from a bygone era.

The survival of People's Sound Records is doubly impressive, for the shop's roots go right back to the 1950s: shop founder 'Daddy Vego' (aka Von Barrington Adams) was a Jamaican national who had been resident in Notting Hill since 1956. He was one of the pioneers of sound system culture in the UK and promoted and supported the development of reggae music across his long life. He was the original 'selector' for the UK's first sound system, subsequently DJ'ing for seven years at the Roaring Twenties Club in London's Soho. Founding his own sound system and calling it People's Sound led to him opening the record shop. Even after his passing in 2016, People's Sound Records has continued to trade and, every Notting Hill Carnival, sets up a sound system out front to blast tunes.

When Vego first began trading, he was one of several local reggae shops: Lee Gopthal's aforementioned Muzik City operated out of 297 Portobello Road in the late 1960s (changing its name several times over the following decades) while the Ali family had Klik Reggae at 245 Portobello Road (this shop also regularly changed name/stock over three decades of occupancy here).

Riddims.

People's Sound Records on All Saints Road, Ladbroke Grove.

CDs and LPs.

Bob Brooks ran Reggae Revive as a stall, then out of Honest Jon's backroom, before opening his own Portobello Road shop. Dub Vendor opened in a literal hole in the wall opposite Ladbroke Grove tube station in 1980 before expanding to a shop in Cambridge Gardens in 1991. Pirate radio station DBC (Dread Broadcasting Corporation) would squat empty shops to sell records. Sound systems and street parties were commonplace across the summer.

Rent hikes displaced the aforementioned shops, along with Plastic Passion and Intoxica – both focused on collectors of 1960s-era music, rock and folk. Appropriately, the only new record shop operating in the Grove is Blue Groove Soundz. Tucked away in the arcade beneath the Westway at 281 Portobello Road, Blue Groove opened in 2019 and focuses on used LPs (alongside a decent selection of 45s). Its stock is largely US imports, ensuring interesting things can be found (as long as you have the time to dig through the copious piles of records). An engagingly scruffy operation, with records stacked up everywhere, Blue Groove resembles the rough 'n' ready used record shops of yore while charging twenty-first-century prices.

BRIXTON

SUPERTONE RECORDS
LION VIBES
CONTAINER RECORDS
UNIVERSAL ROOTS
PURE VINYL

Brixton is both the heart of the South-West London borough of Lambeth and the epicentre of Black Britain – seemingly this came about due to a shortage of available accommodation for West Indian migrants arriving in London in the late 1940s: thus, many were briefly housed in air raid shelters on Clapham Common. While the Trinidadians looked to Ladbroke Grove, the Jamaicans headed to Brixton's Labour Exchange and, subsequently, found housing in the area. And where Jamaicans' go so does music.

Not that Brixton was short of record shops prior to the Jamaicans: L&H Cloakes and Chip's Music Box were noted 78 dealers in Granville Arcade (now rebranded as 'Brixton Village'). As with many other high streets, Brixton had a British Home Stores outlet offering all kinds of household goods: this meant they had a gramophone department that doubled as a record shop and the sounds that once made South London swing – light music, crooners, opera, swing, skiffle – were all sold here. The first Black-owned Brixton record shop was Theo's Record Shop, 250 Brixton Road. Opened circa-1955 by Jamaican emigre Theo Campbell, his shop stocked the calypso and mento records (alongside the US R&B artists Jamaicans then loved), while its upstairs space became home to the *West Indian Gazette* in 1958. Claudia Jones, a genuine revolutionary, edited the paper (Theo wrote the sports pages) and many noted Black writers (including Donald Hinds, author of *Journey to an Illusion: The West Indian in Britain*, a seminal 1966 text), artists, musicians, activists and politicians would gather in the shop. Supposedly Martin Luther King paid a visit when passing through London in 1964, not long after Lee Gopthal, the Jamaican-born founder of Trojan Records and owner of the Musicland and Muzik City record shops, financed the opening of Desmond's Hip City on Atlantic Road.

Desmond's was run by Jamaican national Desmond Bryant and had a large, illuminated sign hanging outside declaring 'BLUE BEAT CENTRE'. For more than twenty years it served as a front-line record shop for the local community; so much so that, one evening in 1974, a supporter of the National Front (the neo-Nazi thug political party) rammed a car into Desmond's shop front. Desmond's survived what would now be considered an act of 'domestic terrorism', trading for another decade, and exists today as the stuff of legend, a record shop as sonic temple.

In 1967, Joe's Record Centre opened in the nearby Granville Arcade, again financed by Gopthal. This time, Joe Mansano, a Trinidadian, was manager and he soon had his own record label, Joe Records (a Trojan offshoot). Here Mansano produced a series of 45s that appealed strongly to ska-loving skinheads and the *Brixton Cat* LP (the first album to feature a Brixton street scene cover).

Music Specialist opened near the station – the owner's son JT continues to run Music Specialist in Tooting Broadway Market today – and other small record shops traded (alongside grocery stores and hairdressers stocking ska and rocksteady 45s). Half a century ago, music was the only media available for Black Britons to openly express themselves and Brixton's record shops proudly did so, often placing speakers on the street to blast new tunes from 'back in the yard'.

David Bowie mural, Brixton. (Photo by Garth Cartwright)

Reflecting a bleak political/social climate in Jamaica and the UK, Jamaican music got heavier and embraced dread, across the 1970s. As the ska shops closed, others opened in and around Brixton: rocksteady singer Alton Ellis ran All Tone's Records in the Granville Arcade for many years, largely trading in Jamaican music from the era when he was king. When I settled in Brixton in '95 the dapper don could often be seen presiding over things; a cool ruler indeed.

A bit further down Coldharbour Lane sat Blacker Dread, a shop as heavy as its name implies. Best of all was – and is – Supertone Records on Acre Lane, a gem of a record shop. On Brixton Road sat Red Records, a shop focused on funk/rap/R&B: by the 1980s, many young Black Britons preferred US sounds.

The record shop crash of earlier this century saw both Red Records and the nearby Our Price close. Alton Ellis died in 2008 and his passing would lead to the inevitable shutting of All Tone's. A few years later, Blacker Dread went to prison for money laundering and his ominous dub shack closed. The stalls and small shops grew fewer. By 2015, only the mighty Supertone Records was still standing. A perfect place to start our Brixton sojourn.

Sound System Sauce and Saxon Sound tapes. (Photo by Garth Cartwright)

SUPERTONE RECORDS

Situated at 110 Acre Lane – on the busy road that leads from Brixton towards Clapham – Supertone Records has changed little over the decades. Entering, you find quite a narrow space with a long, high counter running almost the entire length of the shop. Vinyl 45s and LPs cover the walls, all of them protected by plastic bags. There are racks of LPs and CDs. Posters advertise upcoming concerts, dances and community events. Out the back I spot a room with walls of records – many a record collector would moan at the sight of all these historic 45s. Behind the counter stands Wally Bryan, an affable Jamaican whose warm, witty manner makes him appear far younger than he actually is. 'I closer to 80 than 70,' says Bryan, when I express surprise at his fifty plus years of engagement with Jamaican music.

Wally started Supertone as a sound system, playing out all over London – and further afield – way back in the 1960s. Today he still runs Supertone Sounds – 'for big people dances' – but it is his record shop that keeps him busy seven days a week. In classic Jamaican tradition, Supertone stays open late – often until 9 or 10 p.m. – and locals are always dropping by to chat and listen to music. It feels like a community hub, in the best sense.

Bryan runs his own label where he licenses and re-presses small runs of 1970s-era reggae singles for which, via his shop, he is aware there is demand. Alongside reggae LPs, singles and CDs, he also sells R&B, gospel and 'big people' music (Elvis, Jim Reeves, Charley Pride, etc.), and tickets to Jamaican concerts, dances and dinners. Supertone is a stunning record shop and has been hired as a backdrop for TV and films, and Bryan is one of the nicest guys in the business.

WALLY BRYAN

'1983 is the year I opened Supertone, but it was not my entry to the music industry. No, I've been in the music industry ever since I a youth. I born and raised in Jones Town, Kingston, and while there I become a dance promoter. Coxsone, Prince Buster, U-Roy, I done plenty in Jamaica!

'I come to England in 1964 and, at first, I didn't work in music here. In 1969, I decided I'd left music for too long and built a sound system. I called it The Mighty Supertone and I play real records, not concentrating on dub like some sound systems. I've played all over England, played in Belgium. I used to play for Island Records, when Chris Blackwell was running Island and they had a sound system in a marquee at Carnival. And I still go out and play with the Supertone Roadshow.

Below: Wally Bryan, Supertone's owner.

'I decided to open Supertone Records in 1983 because things were beginning to change in the reggae industry. Digital was making an impact and this meant the sound systems were being forced to change. My workload cut down. So I owned a record shop. Brixton has always been a good place to come and buy reggae records – Desmond's was a great, great record shop! Dennis Brown had his record shop, D.E.B. Records in Battersea Rise. Acre Lane had Tops Records, a top shop! There were many reggae record shops. Now, along with Music Specialist in Tooting Broadway and Pecking's in Shepherd's Bush, I'm one of the few left.'

Bryan puts Supertone's survival down to his shop's willingness to stock a wide variety of music – 'in Jamaica a record shop stock all kinds of music, I the same. I have gospel, Jim Reeves, soul, lots more' – and their reputation as a reliable mail-order shop. 'Right from the start we did mail order and now we have a website and a Discogs page.'

Talking of survival, I was happy to find that Wally and Supertone survived the pandemic. 'It not so bad,' he says, with the nonchalant grace that characterises this elder statesman of roots reggae. 'I keep the shop open in the sense that if you bought a record you could come and collect it from me. And I sell a lot on the Internet. COVID make Internet sales even stronger. Less people come to shop now we reopen.' He shrugs and notes how the pandemic has battered the music industry. Wally wants to take the Supertone sound system out to play but fears he might not be able to do so for a long while.

While Supertone stocks CDs it has always primarily been a vinyl shop and Bryan says he can tell when a DJ is playing a CD. 'Vinyl has a more positive sound. And the vinyl, it holds value.'

He rages against those who sell bootleg CDs and download illegally. 'It hurts us and it hurts the music! It's theft but no one do anything about it.' Supertone kicks against the pricks by licensing and pressing up limited editions of classic reggae tunes for connoisseurs.

'My customers appreciate that I keep great tunes available. If they are not available, they have to pay too much for them on eBay. I do it legal and press them well. You know when you buy a tune from Supertone you are getting a good record!' Never a truer word spoken.

VARIOUS ARTISTS
SENTIMENTAL LP
VARIOUS ARTISTS
MALE
VARIOUS
STUDIO ONE
VARIOUS LP
WINSTON
GROOVY
INSTRUMENTAL LP
KEITH HUDSON
B.B. SEATON
PRESSURE DOWN
PHIL (Bumpy) DINO
CRAZY LOVE -
CRAZY FEELING
Jahug
HEALING
GOSPEL LP
VARIOUS
CAMDEN
The
Country
Side Of
JIM
REEVES
Sanchez
Frankie Paul

Capleton
TWINKLE BROTHERS
Elisha Laverne
DR. ALIMANTADO

Wally has known many legends of Jamaican music over his long life – 'I grew up next to Trench Town. Bob Marley was a friend. Alton Ellis, too! Many visit Supertone.' – and as he says this, Norman Grant of the Twinkle Brothers, one of the great roots reggae bands, walks into the shop. The two men are obviously old friends and the ambience of Wally's shop is very much that of a community hub.

Does, I ask, Bryan have a favourite artist?

'Dennis Brown. No one sing like Dennis. He truly the best.'

Supertone attracts all kinds of customers, from Jamaican pensioners re-purchasing the records of their youth to teenagers who have recently developed a passion for the Caribbean groove. Bryan is proud of his achievements and Supertone's international status. 'Tell them when they come to England to visit Supertone,' he says. 'We are the real deal!'

He is indeed and I've found everything from Burning Spear *Live In Paris* through to classic Studio 1 and Treasure Island and Equals 45s here.

Norman Grant, leader of the Twinkle Brothers.

LION VIBES

Today, Brixton is in a state of flux with ongoing gentrification (spurred by an elite group of super-posh, parasitic landlords who have purchased many commercial properties), leading to local residents protesting over being priced out of a neighbourhood some have lived in since birth. The rebranding of 'Brixton Village' and replacement of small, long-standing businesses with chic cafés and restaurants is a moot point. This noted, Lion Vibes – a small reggae shop – opened in the 'village' in 2016 (proprietor Matt Downs has had a long vinyl connection with Brixton), continuing a tradition of Jamaican music being sold in the Arcade for more than half a century.

Nearby is Pop Brixton – essentially, a selection of chic bars/restaurants and Container Records (yes, all are in former shipping containers).

CONTAINER RECORDS

Jack Christie founded Container in late 2015, having previously sold records online and run the techno record label THEM. Container initially specialised in contemporary dance 12s (new and used) alongside a selection of miscellaneous 45s and LPs. Post-pandemic and Christie admits that with clubs remaining closed DJ demand for hot wax has declined and he's now finding renewed customer interest in classic rock LPs. Thus, Container's back wall has *Paranoid*, *Ziggy Stardust*, *Rumours* and such. Behind the counter hangs new grime, techno, dub step 12s, ensuring Container keeps its groove.

Lion Vibes, Brixton Village.

Staff member at Container Records.

JACK CHRISTIE

'We've had some great parties here,' notes Christie of pre-social-distancing times. 'There would be people dancing and other people buying records. It was a blast!' He looks forward to the day when a small shop like Container can again pack people in but admits that developing into a 'hybrid shop' has been a positive development as it extends the range of records here. On the afternoon I visit, he is sorting through punk bootlegs and Russian pressings. I find soundtracks to Hammer horror and John Wayne films that satisfy my quest for offbeat movie LPs.

'We hadn't been open long when David Bowie died,' says Christie, 'and Sky News turned up with Glen Matlock of the Sex Pistols to do an item on Bowie being born in Brixton. I guess the other record shops in Brixton are focused on reggae, so they came to Container and, fortunately, I did have Bowie LPs in stock so they filmed Matlock buying several. There, we're part of Brixton legend!'

UNIVERSAL ROOTS

Exiting from Pop Brixton, you are close to Electric Avenue – known internationally via Eddy Grant's huge 1983 hit celebrating this very street – where Brixton Market thrives. This is a different Brixton to that of Pop and Village, with Afro-Caribbean and Asian traders selling fresh produce and cheap textiles. And, just a hop, skip and jump from Electric Avenue is the Reliance Arcade, which leads through to Brixton Road. The traders in here have only a small amount of space to operate in but there's often been a record or CD bar and, right now, Universal Roots Records stocks a range of new and used vinyl alongside other merchandise.

Universal Roots focuses on reggae but, within its confined space, also sells used pop, soul, punk and whatever else comes its way. When I arrive, dub is booming out from the speakers as proprietor Markie Smith (aka Jah Lingua) spins tunes. Markie is a friendly chap, and the walls are covered in records and images – many of which celebrate legendary Brixton record shops: there's Desmond's and All Tone and an advertisement for Joe's Record Centre's tenth anniversary. Nice to see what might well be London's smallest vinyl vendor celebrating Brixton record shop history.

(Photo by Garth Cartwright)

Universal Roots' manager and DJ, Markie Smith. (Photo by Garth Cartwright)

'Brixton has always been where people came to buy Jamaican music, so we put the photos up to pay tribute to what came before us,' explains Smith. He then tells me how he grew up in Shropshire before landing in Brixton aged 16 in 1981. This was life changing, with Markie being exposed to reggae and dub for the first time. A lifelong record collector and DJ – he even DJs 78s, mixing between two portable gramophones! – Smith also runs Universal Roots record label, issuing new recordings. A recent release is 'Brixton Downbeat'/'Acre Land Dub' by R.D.K. Hi-Fi, featuring the Soothsayers Horns. Markie plays this 12 and it booms through the arcade, heavy yet light.

I'm impressed by how he runs his record shop and label and also works as a freelance gardener. Did I buy a copy of 'Brixton Downbeat'? Well, of course!

(Photo by Garth Cartwright)

Pure Vinyl's owner and DJ, Claudia Wilson.

PURE VINYL

Universal Roots took over the space from Pure Vinyl Records, a shop set up by local DJ Claudia Wilson. Claudia is Brixton born and bred and well known for her ability to source great reggae, ska and soul records (she began by running a record stall in the Granville Arcade). Pure Vinyl was a friendly place to shop and caught the return-to-records mood that found many young people now buying old vinyl. So much so that when the historic Department Store on nearby Ferndale Road was refurbished and reopened (after decades of neglect) in 2017, Wilson was offered a shop there. She rose to the challenge, shifting from the tiny Reliance Arcade to the Department Store's high ceilings and polished wood floor.

Claudia has the air of a matriarch, admittedly a very warm, welcoming one. A couple of teenage girls drop in and ask if she sells record players. She doesn't, so we direct them to Richer Sounds.

'It's great to see the young loving records again,' she says, 'not just listening on their phones. A 13 year-old girl recently bought a 45 from Mark so he asked her why she liked records and she replied, 'Because it's mine!' That's so true! Love your records. And love your record shops!'

Pure Vinyl has an impressive selection of new and used albums plus hundreds of 45s (largely soul and reggae). Wilson's experience as a DJ ensured she, pre-pandemic, hosted regular events here: open decks on every second Thursday of the month alongside a night in The Ritzy cinema's magnificent upstairs bar on the first Sunday of the month. Brixton was second only to Camden for live music, from the Brixton Academy to the Effra Tavern, Hootenanny, Blues Kitchen and beyond, I regularly caught both touring artists and local talent: Big Joe Louis, Errol Linton, Wizz Jones, jazz, dub, even East European klezmer bands … those were the days. Pure Vinyl captures the essence of a great record shop, bringing people together to celebrate music and community.

CLAUDIA WILSON

'I'm Brixton born and bred,' says Wilson. 'I grew up on Brixton Hill and have lived on the Angelltown estate for the past twenty years.' She pauses, then says, 'Angelltown is notorious today due to gang violence. The media coverage gives it such a bad reputation – they forget that we have a community there.' Wilson grew up buying pop and soul records from a tiny – 'smaller than Universal Roots!' – record shop whose name she has forgotten on Brixton Hill. Having an older brother who liked reggae meant she would often meet him at Desmond's Hip City – 'I was like 9 or 10 and that's how I got reggae on my brain' – while her older sisters turned her on to soul music. Claudia and Markie spent years on the road with his sound system before building her rep' as a soul DJ at Mango Landing, a bar that once stood on Brixton Water Lane.

'I called my DJ nights Pure Vinyl and, as it was all happening at the Mango, we decided to do a Saturday market – that's how I came to sell records. This led to me stalling in Granville Market. My friend was running Music Temple, the record shop that replaced All Tone, but he had real problems and couldn't keep the shop open, so I did a stall to help. Then I got my little

shop in the Reliance Arcade and I just loved it. When I retire from this big shop I'll be happy to go back to that one.

'I came to the Department Store because the business behind it wanted to get local traders in and communicated with Brixton Neighbourhood Forum and they recommended me to run a record shop. I was wrenched to be leaving my little shop, but Mark decided to keep it going and this space is much bigger so allows me to put lots of events on. Locals are our support and I keep things low and friendly. We have open decks DJ events and young jazz musicians come and play in here because they can't get anywhere else in Brixton to make music – the bars all want music and musicians who encourage a lot of drinking. That's not jazz! I want this space to support youngsters – there aren't many places in Brixton you can walk into with no money in your pocket and enjoy yourself. Pure Vinyl is a community space – I worked with the youth when my girls were small, and I know how important it is for them to have places where they can be encouraged.'

Brixton may be changing – property developers are intent on gentrifying the neighbourhood – but Pure Vinyl, Supertone, Lion Vibes, Universal Roots and Container Records (and Soul Proprietors: a small used record shop heaving with vinyl, a good 20 minutes' walk towards Streatham, at 64 Elm Park SW2 2UB) all ensure the community retains its loud, proud soul.

PECKHAM & CAMBERWELL

RAT RECORDS
MAESTRO
RYE WAX
PECKHAM SOUL

I first landed in South-East London in 1994, having met a Spanish señorita (no, not Quintina!) who was based in SE5. There's no tube after Elephant & Castle, so this huge chunk of London was previously unexplored by me (and most other Londoners who didn't live here). It was something of a revelation: Camberwell and East Dulwich were almost village-like in their quaint, scruffy sense of isolation, while Peckham and New Cross had a raw energy, areas where you had to watch your step. Southwark, Lewisham and Bermondsey offered plenty to explore and experience. Yet, one thing was missing: record shops.

Back then, there was A1 Records on the Walworth Road and little else. A1 had a historic pedigree: it opened early in the twentieth century and went on to run its own A1 record label (scoring a Top 10 hit with the late Steve Walsh's club anthem 'I Found Loving' in 1987). By the time I started frequenting A1 – it was situated next to East Street Market and, back in the boom days, apparently used to run one (sometimes two) record stalls in the market – the good times were over, and the shop focused on lamps and electrical goods, its music section having been downsized to a small record bar tucked in the back. Inevitably, it closed for good before the century was over.

Camberwell only had Woolworths, while Peckham had Reeds Music Centre, although this record shop off Rye Lane appeared to be rarely open. If I did want to find music without heading to Brixton or Soho, I would travel to Greenwich, where the outside market (now demolished) had a handful of stalls selling used LPs and cassettes and the indoor market had a discount CD shop. Think about it: the high street record shops were vanishing long before Napster, Spotify and Amazon took hold.

Things hadn't always been this way. Peckham had once been celebrated as a veritable Mecca for both music halls and shopping. Prior to the Second World War there was the huge Jones & Higgins department store – home to a celebrated gramophone department – while Rye Lane was known as 'the golden mile': across the weekend its streets would be heaving with people. Researching *Going for a Song*, I found that, where now stands the wonderful Persepolis Persian café on

Peckham Road, had once been the Peckham Gramophone Store.

Peckham was one of London's most heavily bombed neighbourhoods during the Second World War; this caused huge damage to Jones & Higgins and many other shops on 'the golden mile' and led to the subsequent rebuilding of Peckham with huge council estates. Inevitably, the neighbourhood's character changed and, by the 1970s, Peckham had several reggae record shops, reflecting the new Jamaican community.

One of these was Intone, a shop the late Radio 1 DJ and taste maker John Peel would regularly frequent (he then being surely the only music media guru who ventured down to Peckham to discover new records). Dub Vendor first opened in Peckham (but didn't last long here – the youths running it arrived one morning to find thieves had stripped the shop of everything). The Dub Vendor duo returned to selling records at markets before opening a shop in Clapham Junction and another in Ladbroke Grove. Reeds Music Centre finally closed after its proprietor was robbed and brutally beaten one afternoon. Peckham might be getting gentrified now, but from the late 1960s until the first decade of this century its reputation was that of an impoverished, gang-plagued, knife crime wasteland.

Lee Perry
the
BLACK EMPEROR
Vol. 1
(Vocals)
7" Singles Recorded at Black Ark Studio

Rat Records, Camberwell.

RAT RECORDS

Things began to change when Rat Records opened in Camberwell in the late 1990s. Proprietor Tom Fisher delivered fresh stock (used LPs, 45s, CDs) weekly, all at very reasonable prices. He immediately attracted regular clients and one of them was me. Actually, I spent so much time and money in Rat I began working there part-time. You won't find me behind the counter today, but I do still drop by regularly and often find treasure: purchasing Bobby Charles' Bearsville LP helped me get through lockdown 2. Staffed by Philipe and Andre, Rat sells a very wide selection of vinyl/CDs at extremely reasonable prices. Until lockdown, fresh stock was racked every Saturday morning, attracting queues of diggers (social distancing means that having dozens of diggers crammed together is not viable right now). Rat Records is a gem of a record shop and Tom Fisher spoke with me on the week it reopened.

TOM FISHER

What inspired you to go into the used records trade?

'I was buying and selling on a market stall when I was 20 – thirty-one years ago. I just wanted to get some money to buy more records, so I had to sell some of my records first. I graduated to a tiny shop in Greenwich in 1994. First of three I had there, short term. I went to Camberwell and the current shop in 1999.'

I recall when I first started using Rat there was used vinyl, but its main trade was in used CDs?

'That was when CDs were the future. Dire Straits with no surface crackle – what could be better? I'm happy with either format but at the time all the demand was for CDs. When we opened in Camberwell it was CD only. It didn't work, I went broke, put my own records for sale in the basement and off we went again.'

When did you notice the shift towards vinyl?

'There was always demand for vinyl in the late '90s, tailing off until about 2012, but it was based on the format being cheaper second-hand than CD and unchanged demand for rarities and collectables at a reasonable price. What then happened was demand for fairly standard artists on vinyl started to come back as customers felt that music on vinyl was more 'authentic' and connected to them. Partially as a retro throwback, partly because humans like possessions. But there is not mass demand for vinyl from new artists. The demand is for special editions from new artists and classic retro albums.'

Rat constantly has fresh stock – how do you manage to keep getting a new supply of old records?

'My current Sprinter van has 208,000 on the clock! Basically, a lot of contacts, a lot of driving to buy nationwide, and a fair buying policy. If you want to sell one record, put it on Discogs at the right price. You don't need a dealer. A couple of hours' work for you. But what if you want to sell 300 records, very mixed? You need me, because I'm providing a service; I am collecting them from you, paying a fair price for the lot and taking them away. Hopefully with charm and style!'

I find many used record shops – including charity shops – now overprice any old tat. Rat Records doesn't. Thanks for not treating us as mugs.

'At the shop we have a really, really accurate idea of what a record will actually sell for – it's real worth on the open market based on demand, history and desirability and the opinion of the three of us. We then price it accordingly. We are buying and selling tens of thousands a year. I want to sell records, not look at them.'

What are your thoughts on the future of London record retail?

'It's over. Record shops will go back to a slow but steady decline. The high water mark for us was the end of 2018. Customers get older and buy less vinyl. How many people, struggling to pay rent or a mortgage, need to spend £8 buying *Rumours* on vinyl when they can stream any quantity of almost anything for £4.99 month? The tide is ebbing, but we will see the best-run shops hold on in areas with cheaper rent. A declining customer base, but there will always be some, and it will be for the better, more specialised titles.'

Has lockdown exacerbated this decline?

'Post-lockdown, less people want to shop physically, more people want to shop online. Then you have a recession coming and less disposable income. You need to pay rent and the associated costs to run a shop, and you need staff. If you sell the same stock online, you have less overheads. But only stock with value and a real likelihood of selling. Many of the people who run shops are in their fifties and sixties and they will look at easier, less risky options than a physical shop.

'That noted, I'm not quitting. We refitted the shop over lockdown to make it clean, safer and more pleasant to be in. Crucially, we will have new racking, allowing us to put out twice as much vinyl but we will keep our prices the same. Basically doubling down on our existing model, which our customers like. I would put our chances of being economically viable at the end of the year at 65/35 in our favour. The factors outside our control – recession, financial confidence, virus resurgent, Brexit – will probably decide it rather than what we do. We are just going to do what we did before, but better.'

Record-cleaning machine, Rat Records.

Michael Fountaine, owner of Maestro Records, Peckham.

MAESTRO

Peckham has followed Brixton in enjoying a record shop revival. Not too long after Reeds finally closed, a youth named Michael Fountaine resurrected the shop as Maestro Records. Since then Maestro has focused on serving Peckham's Afro-Caribbean community. It's a Black music shop and you can find everything here from Jah Shaka 45s through Little Beaver LPs to Whitney Houston and Eminem CDs. New and used records mix together in an enjoyably chaotic manner and there's a real sense of neighbourhood shop here. 'I specialise in Black music – reggae, soul, jazz, funk, rare groove, rap,' Michael says, noting that he's been selling music all his adult life.

'I started out in East London markets. I've been selling music in Peckham for more than twenty years. I was in what's now called Sky City [an indoor market] before it got burned down. Then Rye Lane. When I first set up here it was at the height of the CD boom and there was very little vinyl. Now it's the opposite.'

Britain's Black communities used to always have a shop selling Jamaican music; Maestro's now one of the last shops standing offering old and new reggae releases with a wall full of 45s. 'I used to import my reggae and dancehall 7-inch singles from Jamaica,' says Michael. 'Now they're all from Europe or Japan. I used to charge £3 or £4 for a 45 – now it's £8 or £10. That's too expensive for the old clientele but it doesn't seem to put off the new Peckham people. They come here with wealth in their pockets. That's a good thing!'

Michael believes Peckham used to have up to twenty record shops. 'All the others that used to be here are gone. There were at least eight record shops on Rye Lane. Little market stalls selling African CDs. All kinds of things.'

Why, I wondered, has Maestro survived when all the other shops closed?

'I think my thing is I grew up with a lot of the customers and they still pass through. As do their mums and dads and brothers and sisters and aunties and uncles. I'm a family shop, so a lot of people from twenty years ago still come by.'

Indeed, while we speak, members of the public regularly drop in. Maestro also sells concert tickets, reggae books and Jamaican organic hair/healing oils.

Stock, Maestro.

RYE WAX

For the first decade of this century Maestro was the only record shop in Peckham. Then Rye Wax was opened by Tom Stiedl in the basement of the Bussey Building, catering to the clubbers who frequent the former cricket bat factory now it is one of London's foremost nightspots. Rye Wax shares the basement with a bar and a restaurant – thus, its opening hours of 5 p.m.–5 a.m. and regular hosting of DJ events.

Rye Wax's focus is on electronic music, from popular house to the most experimental sounds being created. If beats are where your head is at then Rye Wax stocks them. That noted, the pandemic has ensured the temporary closure of the Bussey Building as a functioning night club and, as Rye Wax is part of the Bussey's club nights, it has, at time of writing, not yet reopened.

Opening not long after Rye Wax, Do You Records, in the refurbished Sky City Arcade, offered new and used vinyl. Do You was run by Charlie Bones but, as Charlie lived in Hackney and was busy with NTS Radio, he kept his shop open for very infrequent hours. Thankfully, Lorenzo Bandiera, a gregarious Italian national who runs the excellent Fly By Night record label (issuing jazz, soundtracks and library music), took on the lease, renaming the shop Lorenzo's Record Shack. During the pandemic, Lorenzo decided to relocate the Shack to Brockley (a bit further south-east).

Rye Wax, Bussey Building, Peckham.

This proved a loss for SE15, especially as Lorenzo's was my favourite Peckham record shop, his Shack stocking new and used vinyl with an emphasis on jazz, soul, reggae, African, Latin and dance music. What have I found here? Everything from The Soul Brothers Six 'Some Kind Of Wonderful' 45 to mono Charlie Mingus LPs in near mint condition (I love it when people have looked after their records). Lorenzo's an extremely affable host and the Shack would pack with music lovers, all sharing their enthusiasm. He recently became a father for the first time, making him a record shop dad. Considering the quality Lorenzo sources, it's worth the hike to Brockley (Lorenzo's Shack is now trading as Lorenzo's Records Wanted, 260A Brockley Road, SE4 2SF).

Around 2015, Peckham was seen as a 'vinyl hot spot' with around half a dozen record shops complementing the new bars and cafés that had the youth flocking to Rye Lane. Two of these only lasted a couple of years: Yam Records in the K&S Indoor Market on Rye Lane was associated with an Internet radio station/club nights and, in late 2017, decided they would shift the station to an industrial space (and close the shop). Sacred Records on the Friary Road still stands, its window bedecked with bright LP sleeves, but has not done its Saturday-only opening for a few years. Run as a passionate hobby by two close friends, it appears that family matters have prevented them from having the time to reopen Sacred. I often cycle past it, its window still bedecked with exotic LP covers, and wonder about the treasure inside.

PECKHAM SOUL

The newest addition to SE15's burgeoning record trade is Peckham Soul, a shop that has employed several different locations – for a while it operated out of a bakery and then in a pub! – before settling in a space in the Bussey Building, just a minute's walk from Rye Wax. As the name suggests, Peckham Soul celebrates classic R&B while also having selections of rock, jazz, dance, African, Latin, soundtracks and much else. The stock is a mix of new and used, with thousands of 45s filed alphabetically by genre. A range of colourful Peckham Soul T-shirts hang from the walls and are a brilliant branding move. While I admire them, the shop's owner, Scottish soul boy Craig Jamieson, admits sometimes he finds there is more demand for his T-shirts than his records.

Peckham Soul interior. (Photo by Garth Cartwright)

CRAIG JAMIESON

How did a Scot come to run a soul record shop in Peckham?

'By accident. My partner moved here with work and I had to wrench myself from Edinburgh, which is a place I still love dearly.'

When I first encountered you, you were selling used records out of a bakery. Then a pub. Now you have a space in the Bussey Building. How did you navigate the journey from coffee to beer to shop?

'These were just pop-ups where I worked with artisan mates who were doing cool things and asked me if I wanted to be involved in that capacity. As my focus was still mostly on DJ'ing and running the label/shop as an online entity it fitted in as it didn't take up much time. The shop itself was, again, an accident: I was doing all the design work for the label from a studio at the Bussey Building and I basically needed more space for vintage stock. The people who run the Bussey said they had a ground-floor space which I could run as a shop as well as a studio. I thought I'd give it a go. One of the best opportunities I've been lucky enough to be offered and taken.'

You have a line of T-shirts and bags all emblazoned with Peckham Soul. How did you develop the concept of Peckham Soul as a brand?

'Peckham Soul is an idea. And it's a very straightforward idea. SE15 is the most multicultural postcode in the country. We believe that diversity is the spark which ignites creativity and debate, building tolerance and making the world a far more interesting world to live in. We fight to defend this. All the label designs and the eclecticism of the shop's music both reflect and unequivocally promote and defend this premise.'

You sell – and DJ – soul music. Is that your foremost musical passion?

'Yeh, but soul music isn't just Black and made between the '60s and '70s. It's music that moves your heart, wherever and whoever it comes from.'

You stock a great variety of music – how would you describe Peckham Soul's stock? And what percentage is new/used?

'50/50 vintage and new. Personally, coming from a background of collecting original releases, particularly Northern Soul, I love finding originals, but I want to stock great music, whatever its issue or catalogue number.'

Peckham got gentrified quickly around 2015–18, were you concerned that some might see Peckham Soul as yet another outsider coming in to make money out of a deprived neighbourhood?

'What??? I grew up on a council scheme.'

Lockdown and beyond: how has it been for business? And how do you see 2021?

'Great. South-East London is my home and it's made me welcome. The work we've put in building on the belief that a local shop can work if it believes in helping and being there for local people has paid off. The support we've had from our customers has been an affirming evocation of why running and curating a record shop is a precious thing to be able to do. At Peckham Soul we are more than looking forward to growing our local shop in 2021.'

Being a cyclist, I venture out in good weather towards Crystal Palace, where the very well-stocked Sound Vinyl is in the basement of Andy Stem's vintage emporium (28–30 Church Road, SE19), with plenty of LPs and 45s: here, I found Eddie Hinton's *Very Extremely Dangerous* album on Capricorn and my heart skipped a beat. Also of note in the same neighbourhood: Haynes Lane Vintage Market (SE19 3AN) has a densely stocked used record shop tucked

Peckham Soul owner, Craig Jamieson. (Photo by Garth Cartwright)

out back, while Palace Vinyl, 1 Victory Place, Westow Street, SE19 3RW, is one of the UK's foremost dance music shops.

Further south-east in Greenwich there's Casbah Records, a spacious, beautifully laid out shop that grew from a stall in the now extinct Greenwich outdoor market. Casbah largely trades in new LPs, but stocks quality used. Casbah's theme is mod/psyche so if you are after tasty 1960s/70s-era albums and singles (plus all kinds of retro memorabilia) then drop by. There's also a Music & Video Exchange for those who have the time to dig through mountains of used records. A hop – or twenty-minute stroll – away in neighbouring Deptford, newbie dance shop Disc World (Arch 3, Deptford Market Yard, SE8 4BX) is run by Chris and Lewis, two enthusiasts with decades of experience DJ'ing, producing dance tunes and hosting events. Someone who knows described Disc World as London's foremost drum and bass record shop. If you fancy a day out in the suburbs of South-East London, then I recommend heading up to Crystal Palace, dropping down to Brockley and, from there, it's not too far to Greenwich/Deptford (it can be done: 6.9 miles cycling or a series of buses and Thameslink connections).

HACKNEY

ELDICA
HIDDEN SOUNDS
JELLY RECORDS
BBE MUSIC STORE
ECSTATIC PEACE LIBRARY
ATLANTIS RECORDS
TOME RECORDS
STRANGER THAN PARADISE

The age of New Labour/Britpop saw both Islington and Camden quickly becoming unaffordable for anyone not on professional salaries. Hackney, long considered by London's bourgeoisie to be a swamp full of brutal council estates and feral squats, welcomed many of those fleeing inflated rents and, in doing so, experienced a youth-led regeneration with clubs, music venues, art galleries, tattoo studios, vintage clothes vendors, cafés, restaurants and, inevitably, record shops opening: whenever I'm informed there's a new vinyl victualler in town to check out, well, more often than not, they appear to have opened in Hackney.

Admittedly, Hackney is a large borough and, thus, these shops are spread over a considerable distance. While Southwark and Lambeth have also benefited from new record shops opening, these are almost entirely based around Rye Lane in Peckham and Brixton's CBD: you can walk between Peckham's three shops in less than five minutes – and Brixton's five in just over ten. Hackney has no central locus, instead, the emporiums are spread across the borough. To visit them by foot would take, well, a good while.

Southwark, Lambeth and Hackney all are, traditionally, working-class boroughs with long-established Afro-Caribbean and African communities. And all have seen, across this century, a more recent influx of highly visible and often commercially oriented younger white people. 'Hipsters?' Some – identifiable by a uniform often consisting of beards, sleeve tattoos, skinny jeans, trilbies and such – but not all.

Remarkably, the gateway to East London contains more record shops than Lambeth and Southwark combined. Why? I've no idea. It's not like Hackney was, in earlier decades, held alongside Soho, Camden and Ladbroke Grove as a place to spend a day record shopping. Pre-Second World War, the borough was noted for its gramophone shops but today there is little record (beyond 78 sleeves) of Dennant's Gramophone House (106 Ball's Pond Road), Shenstone's (15 Dalston Lane), Agate & Co. (Stoke Newington Church Street), Willmotts (123 Lower Clapton Road) and Seddon's (Roman Road). Today, little is known of these shops – often only the address on a 78 sleeve with the shop front in a grainy black-and-white photo being all that remains.

Back then, Hackney was home to a large Jewish community and many of the record shops catered to them. Indeed, the first Hackney record shop to win lasting fame was Jewish – not that its stock was aimed at the local Yiddish speakers: R&B Records

Noreen McShane opened *Stranger Than Paradise* in 2018.

of Stamford Hill, owned by Rita and Benny Isen, pioneered selling West Indian records at the start of the 1960s (and would go on to operate several impressive record labels). For a quarter of a century, R&B served as North London's foremost ska, rocksteady and reggae record shop. Georgie Fame released his very first 45s on R&B's house label and both rude boys and mods would converge on R&B to get the hottest dance tunes. In a sense, multicultural London started taking shape in record shops like Rita & Benny's.

Where the Isens led many would follow and, across the 1970s, Hackney would be celebrated for a multitude of reggae record shops: Lee Gopthal's Muzik Zone chain operated outlets across Hackney; Stoke Newington was home to sound system DJ Gladdy Wax's celebrated Wax Unlimited and the Third World shop, while Lower Clapton Road had Lasco's Music Den and Regal Records.

Reggae and calypso have deep roots in Dalston – The Four Aces was *the* Jamaican music venue – but, during the 1990s, Jamaican record shops began closing. They were replaced, to some degree, by dance music shops: Wired For Sound (WFS), 393 Mare Street, sold jungle and techno, supplying the DJs who played out on local pirate station Rush FM. I never ventured inside WFS, but a friend who did tells me its upstairs department was staffed by youths smoking skunk (and possibly retailing it – certain dance shops were known for offering under-the-counter provisions).

Actually, the last record shop to serve as a hub for a new London sound was Rhythm Division on the Roman Road. Here was grime's epicentre with every noted rapper, producer and DJ performing (or a customer), while mixtapes and independent releases (on CD and vinyl and DVDs of grime sessions) did a busy trade. 'For a little while, Rhythm Division was the heart of grime,' noted rapper Lady Shocker. 'Everyone went there. Everyone.' Rhythm Division closed in 2010 – the youth were now downloading grime – being replaced by a café. Ironically, the borough's transformation into a vinyl Delphi came too late to save Rhythm Division and it now exists only as an online legend. So be it: here are the record shops that now define Hackney's north.

Ridley Road Social Club staircase.

Below: Shaun Whitbourn models Club Reggae LP.

ELDICA

Eldica, 8 Bradbury Street, N16 8JN, in Dalston, is rooted in the West Indian sounds that shaped Hackney. Selling only second-hand vinyl, Eldica focuses on calypso, reggae, soul, jazz and rap. Not that Andy Westbury, who co-founded Eldica in 2000, is averse to other musical genres. Time spent digging here can reveal all manner of interesting records (an EP boasting 'The Spanish Beatles' fascinates Quintina) and certain easy listening and country LPs make me smile.

Eldica is a small shop but it's jammed with records and other stuff, giving it a truly down home feel: there are lots of cassettes, bits of living room furniture (lamps, chairs, tables), ornaments, vintage toys and such, which reflects Eldica's origins as a used furniture shop – once Andy realised selling old records brought in more business than flogging old furnishings, he chose to focus on such.

'Hackney was a great area for reggae – shops, labels, clubs,' says Westbury as he reflects on his neighbourhood. 'There used to be a reggae record shop in this street back in the '90s. Eldica is named after my mother-in-law, who came from Trinidad to London in 1947 – her husband was known by his stage name of Billy Mo, a calypso trumpeter, who played on the Melodisc sessions here in the '50s, before becoming hugely famous in Germany. So the shop was named in her honour and, originally, my wife was selling furniture and fittings. I started selling records here in about 2003 and, by 2006, it was obvious that vinyl was the way forward. I wanted Eldica to reflect Black Hackney and a lot of what we sell is from local collections. We're one of the few shops that are calypso specialists – ten years ago there was no interest in such, now they fly out.'

Westbury notes that, while Dalston is chic today, he found business better in the days when it was one of London's most downtrodden boroughs. 'I preferred Dalston when it was just Dalston and you had your regular local customers who dropped by every week.'

Of lockdown, Westbury admits he went on Discogs to survive – but didn't enjoy it. 'I just want people to come here and buy the records they want, not to have to deal with all the hustlers and blackmailers on Discogs.'

Now that Eldica has reopened, Andy is focusing on selling records over the counter but, he notes, things are not looking good. 'We rely a lot on international visitors and, right now, there are no tourists in London. The pandemic combined with Brexit has done huge damage – there's just not the foot traffic. Either people return or we are in trouble.'

Co-owner Edwin Pouncey with collectors' LPs and Japanese monsters.

ECSTATIC PEACE LIBRARY

This ominous note sent Tina and I cycling up to Ecstatic Peace Library Record Store (EPLRS) at 96 Stoke Newington Church Street. Ecstatic Peace is a pop-up record shop that has attracted greater media attention than any other independent UK record shop in recent years. This is down to a single ingredient that fires up so much media coverage: *celebrity*. Ecstatic Peace was co-founded by Thurston Moore, formerly the guitarist in American rock band Sonic Youth and, since the break-up of his marriage (and thus Sonic Youth), a London resident, and Edwin Pouncey – a noted cartoonist who, as Savage Pencil, has decorated many album covers (while his satirical cartoons lampoon musicians, music industry tyros, fans, journalists and the rest). Yes, he has illustrated several Sonic Youth releases.

Upon arrival, I'm somewhat surprised that the duo have chosen Stoke Newington Church Street to open on, it now being an extremely upmarket neighbourhood (one in which Moore apparently resides). Then we enter and realise that Ecstatic Peace needs high earners as customers – on the walls are a selection of rare psychedelic and folk albums: the 13th Floor Elevators debut is retailing at £600 while a Dr Strangely Strange LP is £995. There's even a £2k tag on one LP – I was so shocked I failed to note its title. This stock of rare records isn't simply the result of Thurston and Edwin making space in their living rooms, instead they've been supplied by Peter Flanagan, a record dealer who once ran Zippo Music, a psychedelic rock record shop in Clapham in the 1980s. As the aforementioned *£££* LPs are all from the psyche era, I'm guessing they might be from his collection.

This noted, there are lots of US pressings of albums from the 1960s and '70s retailing at a reasonable £12 each, while I find a copy of The Dells' *Musical Menu* for £6 (excellent condition too). This gorgeous slice of Chicago soul would be more at home in Eldica than the psych/alternative rock leanings much of Ecstatic Peace Library Record Store is given over to.

Spikey illustrations by Pouncey cover a rear wall and there's a small amount of Moore material available (EPLRS is, I should note, anything but a temple to Sonic Youth). Considering Pouncey and Moore both made their names as part of a post-punk movement that rejected corporate rock and the objectification of rock stars, there is a dichotomy of sorts going on here; one most evident in a framed poster of those titans of trash rock, the New York Dolls, going for anything but a song at £950. Considering how Hackney was long home to proud working-class communities and the likes of the Angry Brigade and Psychic TV were based here (in a vast number of squats), perhaps EPLRS exists as akin to a conceptual art installation, signifying how what once was marginal and underground is now fetishised by the newly minted.

I met Edwin years ago at a concert by Krautrock band Faust (my only memory of their performance is the band setting plastic alight on stage, the toxic fumes quickly emptying the venue), so I reintroduce myself. He notes how, back in the late 1980s, he worked in the aforementioned Zippo Music in Clapham.

Ecstatic Peace is, then, something of an update. Edwin wants the shop to continue beyond its pop-up origin, but it seems the owners of this building are determined to turn the space into a café/barber shop. 'As if we need another one of either of those,' he mutters.

Thurston is not around this afternoon so I can't bug him about touring with Kurt Cobain or what he thinks of Kim Gordon's hateful memoir. Still, as a fleeting glance into the psyche rock past (and how such music has gone from groundbreaking to a bauble), Ecstatic Peace Library Record Store serves its purpose.

Note: Ecstatic Peace has shifted and continued to trade post-pandemic at 1a Bouverie Road (off Stoke Newington Church Street), N16 0AH.

Additional note: Moore is a regular performer at experimental music venue Cafe OTO, 1–7 Ashwin Street, E8 3DL (a minute from Dalston Junction Station), and while the pandemic rages and live music is difficult to put on OTO are focusing on selling LPs (both from their own label and other boutique labels issuing avant jazz and such). Cafe OTO deserves support, so do drop by.

Until recently Melodi Muzik, at 121 Green Lanes, was London's foremost Turkish music shop: alongside CDs and cassettes it sold instruments (saz, oud, darbuka), football club T-shirts, framed posters of Mecca and more. It closed in 2018. Record shops were once as essential to migrant communities as their restaurants and grocers, but the availability of free music online has rendered almost all such traders extinct.

Bait
and
Switch
Don
Cherry
complete communion
Leandro 'Gato' Barbieri / Henry Grimes / Edward Blackwell
Sun Ra
LED ZEPPELIN

Hidden Sounds Record Shop, partners Francesco Ferrari and Alesandro Porchedu.

HIDDEN SOUNDS

As one business closes another opens, and Hackney is, even post-pandemic, fecund with record shops. Heading back into Dalston we cross the A10 near Dalston Kingsland Station and cycle carefully through Ridley Road Market (alas no longer home to the once omnipresent stalls selling Jamaican reggae and gospel 45s and CDs) to 89 Ridley Road, E8 2NH. Here is the Ridley Road Social Club, a 'guardianship' building (i.e. it has a short life left, so is operating as an arts hub on low rent before being demolished), and on the first floor sits Hidden Sounds, a record shop that only opened in this space once lockdown ended in July.

Hidden Sounds first opened in a Bethnal Green basement in October 2019 but, after less than a year, the proprietors found this unsuitable so went looking for a new location. They found the social club space just prior to the pandemic hitting, a disaster for any new business. Luckily Francesco Ferrari and Alesandro Porchedu are young and agile, surfing the ensuring chaos to survive and trade today. 'We weren't entitled to any government help,' says Francesco, 'so times were really tough. I did manage to do some Internet selling just to keep us afloat'.

As their names suggest, they're Italians – 'We met at Genova University,' says Ferrari. 'Both of us were involved in events and DJ'ing parties. I came to London in 2013 with the idea of studying music but I soon realised that if you want to succeed with your music here then you need to be: a) extremely rich and/or b) extremely talented. As I'm neither, I worked in various jobs including managing Mixed Carriage, a Hackney Wick venue that has been put out of business by COVID.'

Betty Wright live.

Francesco Ferrari in the corner of Hidden Sounds.

They began hosting a monthly Internet radio show on Netil Radio (this continues), and venturing into record shops on their travels inspired them to open Hidden Sounds. They were offered the Bethnal Green basement beneath a café in a block of artist studios but it was poorly thought out by the landlords with neither café nor shop attracting foot traffic. In Ridley Road Social Club they again share their first-floor space with a café – a spacious, well-lit one – and are visible to the outside world.

Hidden Sounds stocks a large selection of used LPs and 12-inch singles plus a decent selection of used 7-inch 45s. It has a selection of new vinyl releases – largely from local producers making dance music. Being Italian, they have a great selection of music from across Europe as well as a decent selection of soul/funk/jazz/rock/folk/African LPs. For dance fans they have a large stock of techno and house sourced from DJ friends. Once lockdown's restrictions on gatherings have relaxed, these hirsute Italians promise that they will host DJ events here; they certainly have the sound system required.

Hidden Sounds also sells used turntables, amplifiers, speakers and cassette decks, many sourced via Audio Gold.Their cabinets also stock, alongside new vinyl releases, carving boards designed by an artist and copious quantities of ganja, making me wonder if they had another side business … Francesco smiles wryly, I obviously not being the first to ask, ands says it's THC free, so it is the legal stuff you can't get stoned on. I found LPs here by Betty Wright and Denise La Salle. Here's hoping Hidden Sounds is found by many music lovers.

ATLANTIS RECORDS

Off we cycle to Atlantis Records, along Ridley Road, turning into Dalston Lane, passing Hackney Downs Station, then left into Clarence Road as it meets Mare Street: here sits Hackney's newest record shop, Atlantis having first opened in February.

'Three great weeks and then we had to close,' says John Coxson with a weary sigh. Coxson and his business partner Liam Casey are an agreeable duo; record collectors who have turned their passion into a business. Casey has actually traded in this space for the past nine years as the Pacific Social Club café but was 'sick of serving coffee to people'. He adds, 'When I opened, there were very few cafés around here but now there are loads – so I approached John about turning the café into a record shop.'

Casey's laidback Irish charm contrasts with East London native Coxson, who is quietly intense. He's also a musician (formerly of Spring Heel Jack and Spiritualized). Coxson continues to produce music and runs Treader Records, a label issuing brilliantly esoteric music: the formidable free jazz saxophonist Evan Parker played in Atlantis' window to celebrate the reissue of his great 1978 LP, *Monoceros* on Treader. I was unaware of this event so missed out but, as London returns to a new 'normal', Atlantis hope to host more such events.

'Musically, we're both extremely "catholic",' says Casey. 'I've never met anyone as knowledgeable about music as John. I'm a bit of a magpie – looking at any old junk – I always find stuff!' An example of such is a box of Gujarati 78s on the counter. How, I wondered, did they discover those? Liam explains that he was looking at a photo of speakers on Gumtree and saw a box of records in the background so asked the seller what they were. *Hey presto!* Coxson then notes they also have Yoruba 78s – Atlantis Records is brilliantly eclectic and beautifully decorated, feeling akin to a bar in a port with exotic decorations covering every inch.

'We try and stock every kind of music,' says Coxson. 'We don't want to act like our tastes are superior to yours. We specialise in records! We've even got Russian X-ray records that were made when rock albums were banned by the Soviet authorities. They're terrible but they are a fascinating historic remnant.'

Atlantis certainly has a fascinating selection of LPs, 45s and 78s. Prices vary from the reasonable to those only collectors will pay, but as the shop is so eclectic, it's a pleasure just to dip in and see what's at hand. While I'm there, John shuffles through a handful of dubplates – 45 acetates made only for reggae sound systems and often never issued otherwise (Dalston remains home to a West Indian community). They also have lots of tapes

Atlantis owners, Liam Casey and John Coxon.

Link Wray and Co.

– not just those once sold in record shops but radio and club sessions by the likes of Arthur Russell and Andy Weatherall – plus, plenty of music books. While most of the stock is used, Atlantis does offer new releases on Treader Records (of course) and other, likeminded independent record labels. I find 45s by Huey 'Piano' Smith, Jimmy Reed, Bobby Bland and others to add to my collection although, if I had more time (and money), I could have purchased dozens of items.

'I'm really enjoying Atlantis,' says Coxon. 'We want this to be a record shop where people come and surprise themselves with what they might find. Get a coffee and take your time. We're not selling our records on Discogs because what's the point of having a record shop if you are an online trader? For Treader Records its different – the likes of Evan Parker have fans all around the world.'

Speaking of Parker, Atlantis has started selling his record collection – jazz fan alert! And Geoff Travis' collection, too. From such, Coxon holds up a Jesus & Mary Chain acetate. Not to my taste but, for those who collect them, very desirable.

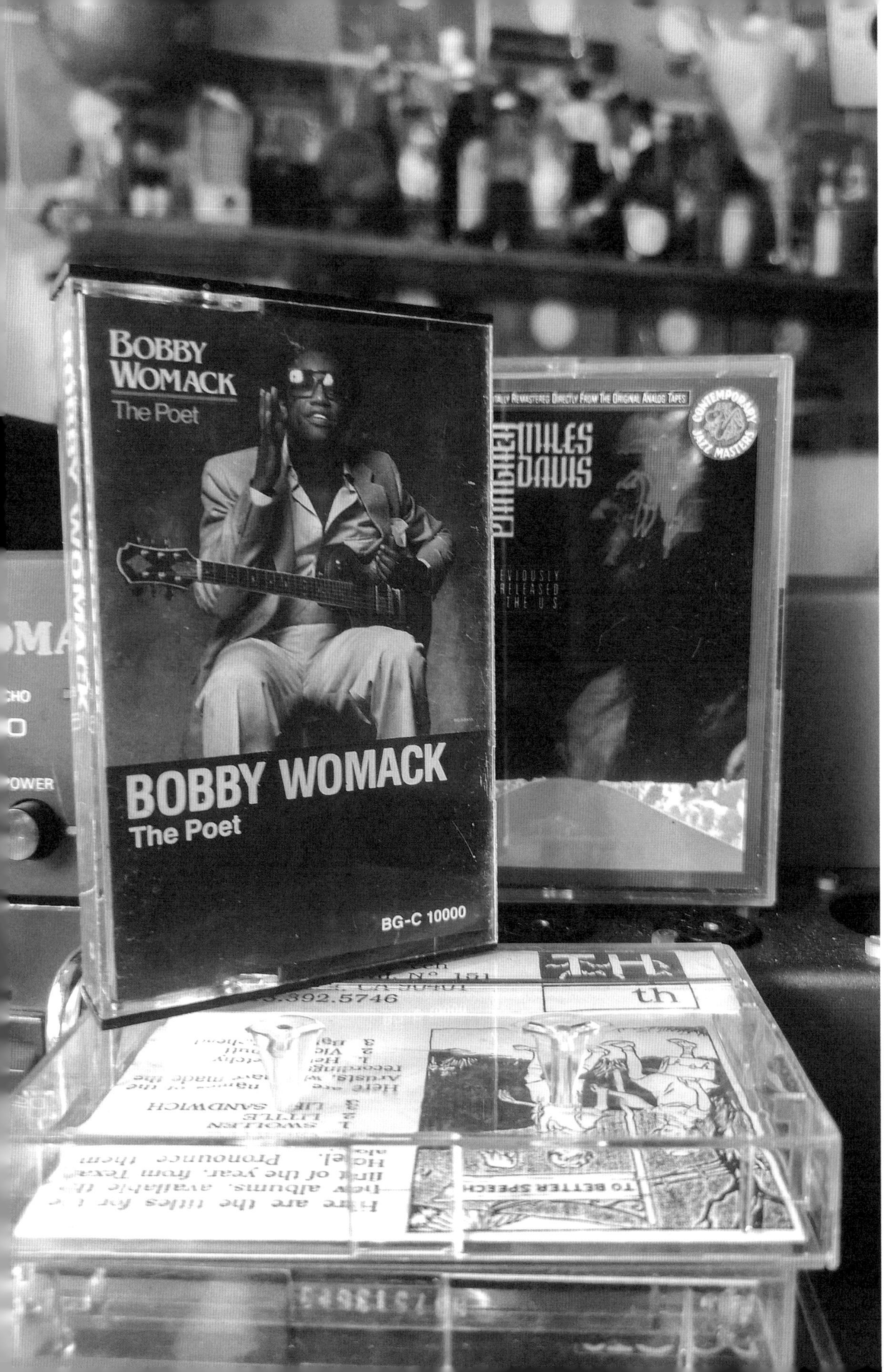
BOBBY WOMACK
The Poet
BOBBY WOMACK
The Poet
BG-C 10000
MILES DAVIS
CONTEMPORARY JAZZ MASTERS
BOBBY WOMACK

Jelly Records, Chatsworth Road, Lower Clapton.

JELLY RECORDS

Speaking of taste, I've not eaten jelly since I was a child, but Francesco at Hidden Sounds recommended that I check out Jelly Records (22 Chatsworth Rd, Clapton, E5 0LP), a shop I was unaware of. Tina and I get back on Dalston Lane, cycling across Clapton Square, taking a few left and right turns until we are on Dunlace Road and then it's a sharp right into Chatsworth, where Jelly sits in the basement beneath a vintage furniture shop.

The stock here is largely used LPs – plus a decent selection of 7s and 12s – and there's lots of everything, from gangsta rap to Japanese pop, on offer. Kev – as the proprietor likes to be known – is a hugely enthusiastic young man who admits he only set up Jelly after purchasing a large record collection and realised selling it via Discogs would be a slow business.

Beyond lockdown shutting Jelly down for three months, Kev says his first year running a record shop has been entirely positive, his winning smile surely encouraging customers to return. Kev is joined in the basement on the afternoon I visit by his girlfriend and their puppy and they are a happy unit. I find plenty of 45s, including an EP by Edmundo Ros & His Orchestra – a 1950s-era fusion of Latin, calypso and pop.

Across the road from Jelly there's a 'ghost sign' of an old gramophone shop that has recently been uncovered. It reads 'Popular Records PARLOPHONE M.G.M PHILLIPS ORIOLE BRUNSWICK DECCA COLUMBIA'. This gets my mind ruminating on the record shop that once stood here, the era it began trading and the era it closed in, its customer base and best sellers. Yes, I'm an obsessive …

Above: Kevin Hendrick, co-owner Tome Records. Below: Kevin Hendrick in front of Tome Records, Graham Road, Hackney.

TOME RECORDS

Jelly Records is the eastern most outpost of any record shop in our London journeys and makes for a fitting border marker. Wood Street Indoor Market in Walthamstow is home to two used record vendors, while the excellent Vinyl Vanguard is at CRATE Building, 35 St James Street, E17 7F. But it's at least another forty minutes' cycle north-east from Jelly – too far for this SE15 cyclist! Instead, Tina and I turn around, tracing our journey back towards Atlantis but, this time, turning left and cycling down Mare Street, then right into Graham Road where sits Tome Records.

Tome is run by Matt Estall and Kevin Hendrick, who used to work together at Flashback in Crouch End, before launching Tome in D.I.Y. Space in Bermondsey (a punk/arts space off the Old Kent Road). Here, they quickly realised that unless there were gigs on there simply wasn't any footfall – D.I.Y. occupied former warehouse space in an industrial estate – and thus they shifted across the river in 2018.

Tome initially specialised in hardcore punk, but it has since opened up to stocking all kinds of music, largely used but also new when it comes to labels the owners believe in. Unlike All Ages in Camden, which concentrates on selling classic punk and hardcore, Tome stocks lo-fi underground productions alongside lots of reggae, soul, jazz and mainstream rock (and much else). They even have an original pressing of Sonny Rollins's *Saxophone Colossus*, retailing for £450 – many a lo-fi, vegan punk band would survive on such for weeks!

'Once we settled in Hackney, our aesthetic changed somewhat,' says co-founder Kevin Hendrick. 'At D.I.Y. we stocked what the bands who played there sold to us as well as lots of underground releases. Here we rely on what comes into the shop from the community and that means lots of reggae and soul. Which makes it, in a sense, organic.'

Hendrick notes that it wasn't Hackney as a record shop Mecca that got Tome relocated from the south-east to north-east. 'I live around here and saw the empty shop – we needed to get out of D.I.Y. so I thought this could work, being on a busy road and just off Mare Street.'

Pre-pandemic, Tome used to hold in-stores with bands but Hendrick says that, due to social distancing, these won't return for a while, 'They used to get so crowded that they'd spill onto the pavement and Graham Road's busy so it's not just not safe.'

UCCI MANE
BOB DYLAN
Merlin Nova
MOLASSES
CONRAD CLIPPER
CYCLE OF LIMINAL RITES
PETER COYTE
Crack & Murmur
MICHAEL JACKSON
DANGEROUS
BEAT DETECTIVES
OXFORD ARDKORE
TOP O DECK
EBENEZER OBEY
Alice Cooper
REGGAE CLASSICS
TOME RECORDS
£ 7.00
£ 5.00
£ 6.00
electronic
ELECTRONIC
PINK GRIP
THE BEATLES
REVOLVER
DETERMINATION
OBEY
chief commander ebenezer obey

Revolver.

BBE MUSIC STORE

Tina leads the way past the Hackney Empire (sadly shuttered as of writing – no panto this Xmas ...), cutting through London Fields and to a back street just off the park. Here, all seem, at a glance, to be former railway arches transformed into restaurants, yet a unit branded The Institute Of Light (seemingly a 'cinema, bar, restaurant, event space & workspace') is an arch where there is a bar, Italian restaurant and, across both sides of the space, the BBE record shop (Arch 376, 10 Helmsley Place, E8 3SB). BBE (Barely Breaking Even) is a celebrated record label that grew out of a 1990s London club night run by Pete Adarkwah and Ben Jolly, who determined that a record label issuing compilation LPs of their favourite jazz, funk, house, disco and hip-hop tunes would be a good idea. So successful were these that BBE began issuing new artist material, the label's biggest-ever seller being J Dilla's *Welcome To Detroit* – one of the classic rap LPs.

On the left-hand side of the arch sit three men at work on their laptops. One is Johnny Reckless, a slim Black guy I immediately recognise as he used to work at Putney's Soul Brother Records (and is a top soul/funk DJ), and there's a young Irishman, Jeff Higgins. They explain that this space is BBE's London base and thus the walls are packed with stock of the label's LPs and 45s.

Black music record labels operating record shops is a long-established practice, with soul and reggae outlets having done so for decades; thus, BBE decided to go into the new space in 2016 with a record shop. Jeff explains that people are welcome to drop by and dig through all the crates of BBE records – plus some second-hand stock – during operating hours. Being in a bar/restaurant space means that people come by to eat and drink and often end up purchasing an album. 'It's a place where people can come and socialise on a Saturday afternoon and hear great music,' says Higgins. 'It's great for the community – BBE is such a part of London's dance scene.'

There are DJ decks in the far corner and as Johnny is a DJ this means the space has hosted album launches, listening parties and other such events. 'Record Store Day is coming up soon,' he says, 'and we will be making a party here – with social distancing.'

Johnny is a record shop veteran, having started work in Record & Tape Exchange in 1987, moving on to managing Reckless Records' Angel shop, then to Soul Brother. 'I like it – all those years behind the counter – and BBE is a totally different animal as we are part of a food and drinks outlet. For me, personally, I think it's the way forward, mixing with other traders – that's better than just struggling by yourself on the high street.'

BBE Music Records is located underneath the railway arches in Hackney

Johnny and Joe, BBE.

Higgins admits the pandemic was a challenge, with the shop closed until restaurants were allowed to reopen. Yet he notes that BBE's website went 'crazy' as fans around the world bought albums. 'Customer confidence for retail shops is not back to what it was pre-lockdown,' he says. 'The amount of people dropping in is less than usual. Obviously, this is a challenge for all retailers – I hope things pick up again. We're lucky, as BBE is primarily a label and the shop is an offshoot, but we love record shops and want all of them to survive.'

'For now, mail order remains our primary way of selling records,' notes Johnny. 'I just posted a package to Stoke Newington – just down the road!'

Being a walk-in customer, I find a KLF 12-inch 45, a Shirley & Lee LP on Imperial and also purchase a brand new copy of Gabrielle Poso's *Awakening* LP on BBE. I'd never heard of Poso, but asked Jeff what the stunning music playing was when I entered and he alerted me to the Italian multi-instrumentalist. Such sonic discoveries are one of the many reasons I love record shops!

Stranger Than Paradise, Mare Street Market, Hackney.

STRANGER THAN PARADISE

While Tina was taking photos, I walked to Sidworth Street – two minutes away – where Lobster Records was situated at No 5. It's not open and nothing on the Internet suggests when it might. Lobster, like BBE, is an extension of the Lobster Theremin record label and specialises in techno and other electronic dance music. Later on, I contact the label and am informed they're unlikely to reopen the shop.

Back on Mare Street, we drop in at Stranger Than Paradise Records in Mare Street Market (117 Mare Street, E8 4RU), STPR is a small shop run by former Rough Trade employees that stocks new vinyl. STPR's love for post-rock/indie and the favourites of such (Can, Kraftwerk, Bowie, Sun Ra) ensures it's an exemplary contemporary rock shop.

I asked everyone working in these North-East London record shops why they thought Hackney was now an epicentre for record shops. Answers varied, but generally they believed the vinyl traders reflected how lots of musicians had settled in the borough over the past thirty years – plus, there's the omnipresent hipster element.

Kevin Hendrick noted how Hackney's record shops are all supportive of one another, pointing customers towards other shops in the borough, and 'this has helped build a network'.

'People who make music gravitate towards Hackney,' said John Caxton.

'It's the new West End,' quipped Johnny Reckless.

All are correct.

BEIGEL BAKE
BRICK LANE BAKERY
No.159
OPEN 24 HOURS 7 DAYS
Tel. 071-729 0616
HOT
BEIGELS
ALL NIGHT
CASH
ONLY

WHITECHAPEL

ROUGH TRADE EAST
FLASHBACK RECORDS
WORLD OF ECHO
CRYPT OF THE WIZARD
YO-YO RECORDS
LOVE VINYL

The record shops in this historic area of East London may cover three different districts – and two different boroughs (Hackney and Tower Hamlets) – but for anyone cycling (or up for a good stroll), they form a loop (of sorts) and all are worth visiting.

While Whitechapel has long been internationally infamous (extreme poverty, waves of immigration, the docks, a certain murderous misogynist) and Bethnal Green had form (due to heavy casualties suffered during the Second World War and celebrity thugs, the Kray twins, hailing from Vallance Road), few people would have heard of Hoxton until it became a byword for hipsters and gentrification in the late 1990s. These days, Hoxton, with its multitude of bars, clubs, art galleries and boutique hotels, is likely more recognised by people under the age of 50 across the globe than Whitechapel and Bethnal Green combined.

Whitechapel has been home to all kinds of remarkable achievements over the centuries and, for this book, it is renowned as where the Levy family opened a record shop way back when. Levy's of Whitechapel – as their shop was known – sat at 19–20 Whitechapel High Street and their 78 sleeves and advertisements always stated that they had been trading since 1890. Thus, let's salute Levy's as pioneers of the record shop age.

Levy's business history always stated how founding patriarch Jack Levy first ran a stall offering sewing machines and bicycle parts, before graduating into recorded music. And graduate Levy's did: pre-Second World War, Levy's of Whitechapel was London's foremost independent record shop, one that claimed, '100,000 RECORDS ALWAYS IN STOCK' and described the shop as 'The House of Music'.

Jazz fans and musicians travelled from far and wide to Levy's, so strong was its stock of what used to be called 'hot music'. Their 78 sleeves also stated, 'All Leading Makes and Languages' – as the Ashkenazi Jewish community in Whitechapel was largely drawn from Eastern Europe and the Russian Empire, the shop likely stocked different titles from these lands. Thus, Levy's would have included klezmer records sung in Yiddish and cantorial records for the religious. Alongside these, Levy's offered records from other areas of the globe – Argentine tangos, Hungarian Gypsy romances, Neapolitan tenors – with much else that made an impression on British listeners in the early decades of the twentieth century.

New Orleans jazz clarinettist Sidney Bechet lived in London for a period in the 1920s and he hung out at Levy's, the Whitechapel shop being London's foremost jazz dealer. Indeed,

Levy's got into promoting jazz concerts and, once Duke Ellington played in London, they advertised that their shop was the only one with a specific Ellington recording available. Ken Colyer, one of the founding figures in the post-Second World War London trad jazz scene, got the 78s from which he learnt his craft from Levy's.

While jazz was the hot new music attracting people to Levy's from across London (and likely further afield), Whitechapel then was largely a Jewish ghetto, its tenements packed with impoverished immigrant families who had fled pogroms across the Russian Empire. Whitechapel, with Brick Lane as its commercial epicentre, was home to Yiddish music halls and many gramophone shops: these sold not only gramophones but the records you needed to play on them.

Unlike Levy's, these record shops never developed into the stuff of music industry legend so not a great deal is known about them. The sleeve of an E. Adler & Co. 78 determines the shop is based at 34 Brick Lane and states that they sell 'Jewish, Hebrew Records'. Among the record labels listed on the sleeve is Emerson, an American label that traded between 1915–27 and had an extensive catalogue of Jewish recordings. Thus, Adler was likely importing Emerson 78s to meet local demand. An advertisement for Weinberg's Gramophone Shop at 138 Brick Lane features almost all the text in Yiddish, the translation of which reveals, 'At Weinberg's you will get the most modern gramophones or gramophone cabinets at the cheapest prices' and 'Before you go somewhere else, come to Weinberg's'.

E. Kominsky's, at 172 Brick Lane, continued selling records until 1977 and is documented as having sold furniture as far back as the 1920s. Kominsky's specialised in gramophones and radios and, as demand for records increased, the family who ran it developed the record department until it became the shop's focus: in the early 1970s, ska and rocksteady fans would head there because it was noted for its large stock of Jamaican 45s, especially those on the Treasure Island label. Vinyl treasure, indeed!

An E. Kominsky 78 sleeve notes, 'Open All Day Sunday' – the Sabbath ensuring they did not trade from Friday evening until Saturday dusk. There's a stunning album detailing Jewish Whitechapel's swing scene – *Music is the Most Beautiful Language in the World: Yiddisher Jazz in London's East End 1920s–1950s* (JWM) – that gathers many fabulous recordings plus historic detail from what is now largely a forgotten era ('Beigels' by Max Bacon is worth the price of admission alone).

It's worth noting that the Levy family were not just successful at running record shops (opening a branch of Levy's in Regent Street). They set up record labels (Levaphone and Oriole) to record local talent (both Jewish artists – religious and secular – and Anglo), scored hits with crooners and skiffle, licensed music from different labels across Europe and the USA (they represented Motown in the UK at the start of the 1960s, then BBC radio restrictions on playing pop records meant Oriole failed to score hits with seminal singles now regarded as Detroit classics), owned a pressing plant and a recording studio and went on to carve out a very profitable niche recording and manufacturing all the 78s (then 45s) for Woolworths' Embassy Records (which specialised in ersatz covers of chart hits by unknown local musicians – these were sold exclusively in Woolies' hundreds of UK shops and retailed at half the price of the original chart hits on EMI and Decca!).

Levy's, by starting out as a record shop then developing into a record label (and beyond), set the template for what the likes of Richard Branson would later do with Virgin and Geoff Travis with Rough Trade. Not that any of the Levy family ever had the high profile the aforementioned record men did (or launched any truly ground-breaking artists). Instead, they got on with business from 1890 up to 1964 (when they sold their empire to CBS – having closed their Whitechapel record shop at some point in the 1950s). Not a bad innings for a record shop that grew out of an East End sewing machine market stall!

When Levy's closed there would have been other merchants happy to pick up the trade: Petticoat Lane Market had several stalls selling records and small record shops abounded (there was even another Levy's – not linked to the aforementioned shop or family). Most are now long forgotten, but one that is spoken fondly of by older Cockneys is Paul For Music. Opened by Paul Shoben at 13 Cambridge Heath Road, E1, in 1954, Paul For Music went on to have two more branches – one in Leather Lane, Holborn, and another in Finsbury Park. The latter became a noted reggae shop in the 1970s.

Most memorably, Paul operated a stall outside Whitechapel tube station every Friday and Saturday. The stall focused on selling ska and R&B so every mod worth their mohair suit made a beeline for it. Paul's son David took over Paul For Music in the 1980s and the Whitechapel shop finally closed in 2005, getting out of the recorded music trade as downloading took hold. That this marvellous record shop survived for fifty-one years of continuous trading is a great achievement.

Across the twentieth century, Whitechapel changed a great deal: the Jewish community shifted north to Golders Green and Finchley, Bangladeshis quickly taking their place. Thus, kosher restaurants were replaced by curry houses while Jewish record shops were replaced by Asian ones: when I first landed in London, Brick Lane was where I would go to buy cheap cassettes from the Indian subcontinent.

Today, there are still plenty of Bangladeshi restaurants and shops selling food and textiles on Brick Lane's southern stretch but the last Asian record shop, Sangeeta Ltd, closed a few years ago (it's now a salad bar). Where Asian neighbourhoods across the UK were once served by prominent record shops selling music from 'home', these emporiums, often ablaze with colour and incense (while Bollywood soundtracks or bhangra beats blasted forth), disappeared with the advent of downloading. By the early 2000s, rents were rising rapidly and hipster cafés and bars began opening in Brick Lane's northern end.

Music is the most beautiful language in the world!

Buy a gramophone or a gramophone cabinet.
And hear the most beautiful music in your own home!

At Weinberg's , 138, Brick Lane, East

You will get the most modern gramophones or gramophone cabinets at the cheapest prices.

Records!

You will find the greatest choice of gramophone records at Weinberg's. Before you go somewhere else, come to Weinberg's, 138, Brick Lane, E.1.

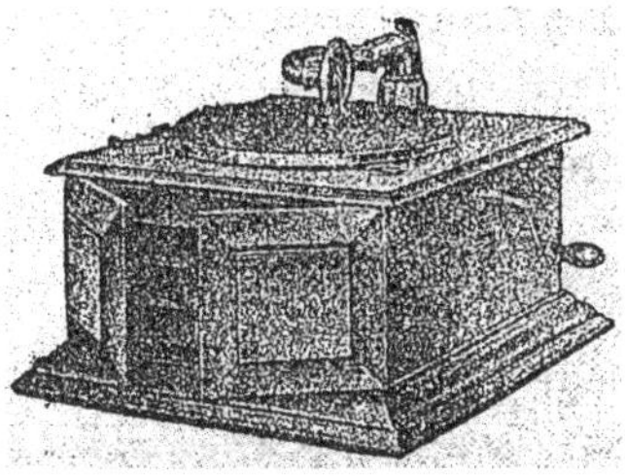

Gramophones!

Buy your gramophones and records at Weinberg's and you will be sure to get the right article for your money.

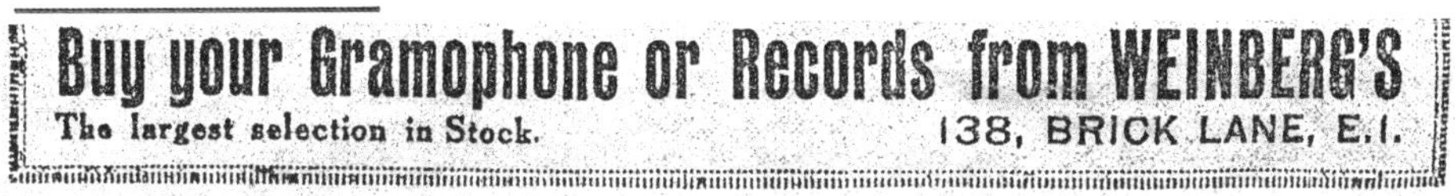

Weinberg's of Brick Lane advertise in Yiddish and English. (Courtesy of Alan Dein collection)

ROUGH TRADE EAST

Nigel House (manager of Rough Trade record shops) was aware of these changes and, having called time on the tiny Rough Trade shop in the basement of Slam City Skates (in Covent Garden's Neal's Yard), decided Brick Lane was the perfect place to open a revolutionary new record shop. Rough Trade East opened in 2007, the spacious shop having a café and live music stage plus plenty of music books on display. Its remarkable success helped to inspire London's record shop revival. Staff that have worked here have gone on to open record shops across London, Margate and Bury St Edmunds, while House has rolled out Rough Trade shops to Bristol, Nottingham and Brooklyn (USA).

'In 2007 we shifted from Neal's Yard to here,' says House. 'It had got to the point where our lease was running out there and the rent had increased to the point where we could no longer justify being in Covent Garden. I'd been wanting to come out here for quite a while and had been thinking about a Rough Trade superstore of sorts – the opposite of Neal's Yard. This is the modern form of Rough Trade – Rough Trade West remains the heart and soul of Rough Trade and exists for the real record nuts. But it is hard for a shop that size to make money. It's much easier for a shop this size to make money because we can have so much more stock and we don't just rely on selling records. It's hard for any shop to survive on just selling LPs and CDs these days because the margins are so small, and you don't sell the quantities you once did.

'When we opened this one some people said, "You're mad!" But our timing was right for this area and has made us at the heart of where a lot of things are going on. Just as Portobello was in the 1970s. That said, the first couple of years here were really tough. We went from having a small shop in Neal's Yard to this huge shop. It's so much bigger that it has more of everything and, when we opened, it was very much still the CD era and they are small, so I realised it was hard to draw attention to new releases. We had the new PJ Harvey album racked when we first opened, and a young woman walked up to the counter and asked if we had PJ Harvey's new album – that really drove home to me how important it was to rack things up in a way they can really be noticed. Now, with the return of vinyl, it's much easier to do that. It took us a year to get things right.

'We occupy a strange area where we have to balance between being an independent shop and something of a chain store like HMV. I like doing things that aren't seen as "Rough Trade". If Taylor Swift was up for doing an in-store, I'd have her in a minute!

Rough Trade East, Brick Lane, Whitechapel.

Staff member Ian holding Ultimate Success Today by Protomartyr.

'Simon Draper, who was one of the co-founders of Virgin, helped out when we were looking for investment. He took us to meet this guy who had a lot of money and, after he had studied Rough Trade, he said, "What you have is not a business but a passion". It *is*. It's about the music, the art. That's more important than selling loads of Phil Collins records.'

House smiles then adds, 'I always loved it. Still do. Coming in and listening to new records is just great and selling it to someone just makes the job perfect. I still find hearing new music really exciting and I hope the kids still find it exciting too.'

I interviewed House a good while before the pandemic forced record shops into lockdown but am aware that Rough Trade's strong profile – both local and international – and website ensured the chain sold plenty of stock during the closure. All Rough Trade UK shops have reopened (with hand sanitiser, masks and social distancing). While footfall in Brick Lane is way down (pre-pandemic, it came close to matching Camden Town as a place that youth and tourists gravitated toward), London's most famous rock shop will surely continue to lead the way.

Flashback employee Lorenzo Perera models Raja Rani LP.

FLASHBACK RECORDS

Cycling up Brick Lane, I stopped at Beigel Bake for a salmon and cream cheese beigel and cheesecake (the two beigel shops being the last vestiges of the Lane's Jewish community), then turned right into Bethnal Green Road. Immediately, I'm at Flashback Records of Shoreditch.

Flashback is an independent chain of three London used record shops: the first is in Angel (50 Essex Road, N1 8LR) and opened in 1997. The next is in Crouch End (144 Crouch Hill, N8 9DX), which opened in 2006. The last, but not least, is the Shoreditch shop, which opened in 2014. Flashback was launched by former employees of Reckless Records and it's a testament to both good management and their ability to source strong stock that they have built their mini chain.

I'm rarely in Angel and never, ever, in Crouch End, but the Shoreditch one is a shop I drop in to whenever I'm in this neighbourhood: it has plenty of interesting LPs, singles and CDs. You need to be patient when heading into a Flashback – there is a huge amount of stock with the bulk being rock/pop/dance music – but surprises can be found here.

WORLD OF ECHO

I make my way back, cutting through Barnet Grove and up to World Of Echo at 128 Columbia Road. Situated where the Columbia Flower Market is held every weekend, this small shop is beautifully designed and laid out. World Of Echo has the atmosphere of a chic art gallery, which is appropriate as it specialises in art rock/experimental music/lo-fi/free jazz and other such genres that *The Wire* magazine covers. Obviously, they have Kiwi customers as it's the only UK record shop in which I've ever found copies of 45s by Blam Blam Blam and The Chills (early 1980s-era New Zealand arty indie bands).

Crypt Of The Wizard's owner Charlie Woolley

CRYPT OF THE WIZARD

From an art rock haven to a metal Mecca is only a very short distance. 264 Hackney Road is where I find London's most exotically named record shop, Crypt Of The Wizard. Yes, you guessed right: Crypt is a rock shop specialising in selling metal. Co-founded by Marcus and Charlie in 2017, Marcus left just before lockdown for 'pastures new' and Charlie now runs the Wizard, having shifted the shop from 324 to 264 Hackney Road.

It's only a short distance and, when I dropped by, Charlie was still setting up shop. He's kept busy over lockdown serving his mail-order customers and, as of writing, was opening only three days a week to serve those who had ordered online and were dropping by to collect their records.

Named after a 1996 album by Norwegian black metal artist Mortilis, Crypt Of The Wizard is London's only specialist metal record shop and one of only a handful of such anywhere. Which is bizarre, considering how metal has been one of rock's most popular genres for the past fifty years and its many splinter sects – black/thrash/death, etc – command extremely loyal fanbases.

Crypt is packed with vinyl, CDs (lots of CDs – metal fans still being happy with this format), cassettes (again, loads of cassettes), T-shirts, fanzines, stickers, badges, etc. For metal fans, the Crypt must be something of a Mecca. Stock is both new and used (although largely new) and, being specialist, ensures the Crypt gets stock of all kinds of limited edition pressings.

Charlie's a hirsute man of few words – preferring to let the music do the talking (or screaming, this being metal) – and his Facebook posts are extremely droll. Here's a taster:

> *A strange sigil hath emerged upon thee Hackney Road, curious and grotesque as if risen from thee very depths. False mystics and seers art divided on what it may portent, but thee true acolytes know it can mean'th but one thing … thee return of thee Wizard is imminent.*

I think this means Crypt Of The Wizard will soon reopen. When it does, and your inner goblin wants to hear the likes of Antichrist Siege Machine, Ulcerot, Bloody Head, United Mutation and other such noise boys that are unlikely to get airplay on radio (or much coverage in whatever music media still exists), then Crypt is the record shop from hell that should sate your cravings.

Drunk In Hell.

Yo-Yo's owner, Derek, DJs.

YO-YO RECORDS

Five minutes' walk from Crypt Of The Wizard stands Yo-Yo Records at 324D Hackney Road. Talk about yin and yang – I doubt a black metal album has ever darkened Yo-Yo's doorway! Yo-Yo's was known until early 2020 as Cosmos Records and began in Toronto, Canada, in 1998, opening in London in 2015. It only sells vinyl, focusing on jazz, funk, soul, gospel, Afrobeat, Brazilian, soundtracks, psych and such.

Much of its stock is sourced from the USA and Canada, Yo-Yo specialising in first pressings that are in great demand. This means the vintage vinyl here can be seriously pricey. That said, there are many reasonably priced albums (and 45s here – I pick up classics by O.V. Wright, James Brown and Lynn Collins and the Isley Brothers here).

Proprietor Derek insists on spraying our hands – as well as the wearing of masks – inside Yo-Yo. He's a friendly Canadian who prefers not to give his surname as he is also a visual artist (and thus keeps his two careers separate). Derek explains how, having married an English woman and having worked for Cosmos in Toronto for a decade, he settled in London only to find there was no equivalent shop specialising in high-end first-edition jazz, rare groove, Brazilian and such. Living on the Hackney Road leant familiarity with an empty shop at 324D and, one day, spotting a small sign in the window as to its availability, he made a call. Site secured, Derek then set about opening Cosmos.

Cosmos quickly gained a reputation as the place where you could find jazz and gospel LPs that no one else in the UK appeared to stock. It was beloved by DJs and collectors and those with a penchant for the extremely rare. Then, in February 2019, Derek and his wife decided to break with Cosmos and set up Yo-Yo: nothing has changed regarding the shop's stock, beyond where it was all supplied by the Toronto headquarters, Derek now sources everything.

'It gives us more freedom – especially in pricing,' he says. 'I think we had a reputation as a bit of an expensive record shop and, of course, we do have some very collectable albums [he shows me a £1,000 LP by Joan Brooks; it's an extremely rare private pressing of an album/artist I've never heard of] but we also now have plenty of affordable albums. I stock LPs by The Police and Gloria Estefan – I'm not a snob! – but I do focus on private pressings of psych albums and rare jazz and funky Latin, the kind of stuff that is really hard to find.'

Most of his stock is used – in excellent condition – but Yo-Yo does stock an assortment of new albums. 'It's all sale-or-return on local labels – Floating Points, Brownswood, etc. Reissues of spiritual jazz and stuff that we love.'

Dakota Gomez digs in Yo-Yo Records.

As with Atlantis Records, lockdown hit only three weeks after Yo-Yo had renamed/reopened. 'We had the best three weeks of our life and then – bam!' says Derek. 'We actually shut before the government told us to as Yo-Yo attracts people from all around the world, so I wanted to take extra precautions. We don't do Discogs – I want people to come here and buy records, not just buying online – but I did set up as an Internet trader and we kept very busy. People actually thanked me for selling records online as they were so wanting to get albums to listen to during lockdown.'

Yo-Yo is brilliant and, if I ever win Lotto, I will purchase a vast number of rare LPs here. For now, well, it's nice to admire original Blue Notes and such.

LOVE VINYL

Then it's a short walk – or a few minutes' cycle – north-west to another brilliant shop, Love Vinyl at 5 Pearson Street, Hoxton. Love Vinyl opened in 2016 as a dual shop, with two partners selling old soul/funk records and two selling new dance music. As enlightened as this seems, it proved unprofitable, with the newbies leaving pre-pandemic. Co-founders Zafar Chowdhry and Jake Holloway now ensure Love Vinyl has a remarkable selection of soul and funk and house and disco. But they also stock LPs by Fleetwood Mac and Jacques Brel and gospel and jazz and much else – this is a record shop aimed at serving all kinds of people and they want it to do so.

Both men have worked for BBE – Chowdhry compiling dance albums, Holloway does all the label's graphics.

'I also run the '80s label with Phil Asher – a top UK house producer,' says Chowdhry. 'Here we still stock some new releases, but they are so bloody hard to sell right now so we are concentrating on vintage vinyl.'

I asked Zafar what he'd enjoyed most about running Love Vinyl and he replied, 'We've had loads of bands and every top DJ do in-stores here – and we've had such a great time doing so! You can find Dele Sosemi's performance here with his Afrobeat brass band on YouTube. It was brilliant!'

Until the pandemic struck, I would have taken a short walk across the A10 to Hoxton Street where M.O.V.I (Matters Of Vinyl Importance) existed for three years. This small record shop/café/bar was founded by two friends and music industry insiders in 2016. They ensured M.O.V.I. put on all kinds of events – live music, author chats, music films (often held at Rich Mix, one of London's foremost live music/art film hubs on Bethnal Green Road) and much else. Then the pandemic hit and M.O.V.I. crashed. Co-founder Alan Pell explained what forced them to shut up shop.

'There were a few reasons. We were struggling with lots of general trading stuff – Hoxton Street Market went downhill very quickly and, despite having several meetings with Hackney Council, there wasn't the will to even think about trying to compete with other "East End" markets. Brexit played a role, lots of City boys with money moving overseas, out of London or losing their jobs. Nowhere near as many foreign students coming by and using us

Above opposite: *Co-owner Jake Holloway DJs at Love Vinyl, Pearson Street, Hackney.*
Below: *Guy Cochrane digs.*

LOVE VINYL
WE BUY RECORDS
TOP PRICES PAID!
Tuesday - 11:30am/6:30pm
Wednesday - 11:30am/6:30pm
Thursday - 11:30am/6:30pm
Friday - 11:30am 6·30pm
Saturday - 11:30am/6:30pm
Sunday - 11:30am/6:30pm

RAY CHARLE
COLLECTION

as their 'local hangout'. Distributors giving Rough Trade East bigger discounts/exclusives – we just couldn't compete on price. And, yes, landlords not giving tenants a break, despite income dropping to zero with lockdown.'

As of writing, M.O.V.I. exists as an online record shop only. A sad ending for one of London's foremost rock shops – the owners like to note that their stretch of Hoxton Street was where The Verve's 'Bittersweet Symphony' video was filmed. The Arctic Monkeys turned up once to shoot a video there, surely paying homage to the Wigan wonders, while also surely wanting to check if M.O.V.I. stocked their latest LP.

Several Hackney record shops bemoaned the August closure of Low Company, a record shop situated in Amhurst Terrace, Hackney Wick. Low Company existed as an extension of a label (Blackest Ever Black) and specialised in underground dance, DIY, industrial, post-punk and such. Its ability to source new records from tiny labels in different regions brought it much praise. 'You'd go in there and hear sounds that you had never heard before,' said Charlie from Crypt Of The Wizard. He added, 'and you'd buy records you never knew you wanted.'

Low Company opened in 2017 and issued a wry weekly newsletter detailing the new releases in stock that helped give the shop a very personal identity. Then the pandemic hit and Kiran Sande, shop and label owner, emailed out a statement in late August noting that the shop would be closing later that week:

We will not be opening the door of our Hackney Downs abode again. And please, we won't be 'pivoting to online-only' – whoever dreamed of running a web shop? If/when I do sell anything via the Low Company site, shipped from my hovel on the soft south coast, it will be sporadically, and grudgingly. To reiterate: THE SHOP IS DONE. It isn't coronavirus that has brought about our particular shopocalypse – I'm not sure anyone will believe me, but I made the decision to shut permanently (by Spring 2021) about two weeks before lockdown was first imposed in the UK – but it certainly has sped things along. It felt pointless to reopen only then to close again in less than a year's time.

And of course, LC as a 'somewhere' doesn't make a lot of sense in the post-COVID-19 shitescape. When all is said and done, I opened a shop purely 'cos I wanted a place in London I could call my own to sit and hold court and drink and have a good moan. Facemasks, visors, Perspex screens, anti-bac wipe downs, social distancing and the constant doling out of hand sanitiser were never part of my shop-keeping fantasies. And toughing out the inevitable next three years of deep recession for the love of music is one thing, but doing it through a gloryhole with a bag over my head? No ta.

As M.O.V.I. and Low Company were among London's most innovative new record shops, their passing casts a pall over the entire trade: can independent record shops survive a recession? Will the HMV chain, having taken a battering over the past twenty years, struggle on? Hard times surely lie ahead. Still, just as I learnt of Low Company's closure I heard of Next Door Records (304 Uxbridge Road, W12 7LJ) opening in Shepherd's Bush. Kingdoms rise and kingdoms fall! I'm guessing there will be new shops in Hackney and other postcodes: the love of music and records endures even the worst of times.

Chatsworth Road gramophone shop ghost sign.

FINAL NOTE

Tough as conditions are for independent traders, record shops operate as creative hubs possessed of a value far beyond simply selling stock. And it is this, their sense of community and engagement with music, friendship, creativity, the odd and obscure, that ensures many of us will continue to show them love. At their best, record shops represent an underground empire that traffics in joy: here, inspiration and imagination, trade and pleasure all coalesce. I hope these sonic temples survive and thrive – London remains the world's record shop epicentre and these maverick vendors of black metal and funky jazz, old soul and new reggae (and much else), help ensure this city remains inspired and inspiring.

The rapacious nature of late capitalism has blitzed the high street until all that's often left standing are charity shops, pound stores, chicken shacks/burger sheds, chain outlets and empty spaces. Amazon, Tesco, et al. take their profits offshore and leave a wasteland that contributes only to our spiritual and social impoverishment. Contrast the independent traders of, say, Totnes (or Belsize Village) with, say, Camberwell Green (a supermarket/pound store/charity shop/junk food hub – Rat Records being its saving grace) for evidence of how corporate capitalism impoverishes our communities. So, you say, what can we do?

What indeed: as consumers, one of the few powers we have is to refuse to spend money in outlets that, essentially, pimp our neighbourhoods. Support local traders and street markets and show some love to local (and not so local) record shops. And get off your computer and shop among your fellow humans or else … how's the Joni tune go? 'You don't know what you've got 'til it's gone …' Well, indeed.

This includes distancing from both music-streaming sites (few musicians are properly remunerated by such) and websites designed to make record collecting easy – indeed, too easy. They are also increasingly full of sellers looking to overcharge on both records and postage. These Internet shopping sites are not just bad for your bank account, they're bad for your health, encouraging isolation and deadening the imagination, lacking any element of surprise or engagement. Go for a dig (and amaze yourself at just what you might find), have a chat, sample the coffee or beer (if they sell such), buy records and cassettes and CDs (and books, T-shirts, etc.), attend a socially distanced event, listen and learn and enjoy and engage. Record shop retail therapy enriches life. As Weinberg's of Brick Lane once averred, 'Music is the most beautiful language in the world!'

Unexpected kindness is the most powerful, least costly, and most underrated agent of human change.

Bob Kerrey

ACKNOWLEDGEMENTS

Thanks to Nicola Guy at The History Press for commissioning *London's Record Shops*.

For their support and help in gathering historic information on the gramophone-era shops, I should single out the City of London Phonograph & Gramophone Society (CLPGS) – Tom Stephenson and Roger Mackay especially. The CLPGS was founded in 1919 and is dedicated to the research of all recorded sound. Its quarterly magazine *For the Record* is a font of information on the gramophone era and is highly recommended (www.clpgs.org.uk).

Alan Dein is an expert on Jewish London and his help on the Brick Lane gramophone shops was invaluable, he even translated Yiddish advertisements when I requested such.

Ben Ayres & Tjinder Singh of Cornershop make brilliant music: I'm honoured they wrote the foreword for this book.

Not having any family in the UK, my friends here fill that space. Many thanks, then, are due to Errol Linton (and band); Bonnie Dobson, Petar Zivkovic, Marc Engel, Carina Westling, Conrad Heine; Taib Akri, Tony, Ted, Roger Neil @Ace Records; Richard Marshall, Adrienne Connors, Graham Robertson, Big Joe Louis, Cheikh Diane, David Katz, Nick Nasev, Ian Bailey, Steve Barrow, John Williams, Martin Morales, Gareth Evans, Rob Hackman, Dr Sophie Faroque, Andy Jones, Wilson's Cycles, Tim Everson, Yvonne Deutch, Phillip Minns, Brian O'Neill; Meg, Merit, Cigdem and all at She'Koyokh. Socially distanced hugs to amigos in New Zealand, USA, Spain, Berlin, the Balkans and elsewhere. To any pals I've overlooked – I owe you a pint …

Ta to the publications who gave me space to write on my myriad enthusiasms: *The New European*, *Songlines*, *Vive Le Rock*, *Jazzwise*, *The Guardian*, *Rock 'N' Reel* and *Long Live Vinyl* (sadly RIP).

A big shout out to Robert Elms, Gilles Peterson, Gideon Coe and Cerys Mathews for their celebratory BBC radio shows.